CHARACTER ENCYCLOPEDIA
UPDATED AND EXPANDED

Written by
Claire Sipi

CONTENTS

WELCOME BRAVE NINJA

The LEGO® NINJAGO™ world is full of adventure, danger, and epic battles! Meet the four ninja: Kai, Cole, Jay, and Zane, and the unlikely hero Lloyd. But that's not all! There is a new ninja on board with exciting powers—Nya! Join them on daring and dangerous adventures, as they battle fierce enemies all seeking to rule Ninjago Island. Read all about the ninja's amazing elemental powers and their mighty weapons as they fight a host of bad guys, from the dreaded Skeleton Army to Nadakhan the djinn and his crew of Sky Pirates. Helping them to battle evil are some powerful allies, from wise Wu and Misako to fickle Ronin. After all, an adventure is no fun without friends. Go ninja, go!

To find out more about this minifigure see p.194.

HOW TO USE THIS BOOK

This book is a comprehensive guide to every LEGO NINJAGO minifigure released so far. Divided into seven chapters chronicling each season of the TV series, NINJAGO™: Masters of Spinjitzu, the book covers the adventures of our heroes from the TV pilot to the latest 2016 season. Each chapter provides detailed information of all the minifigures that appear in the season. Discover the likes and dislikes of each character, learn all about the new abilities that the ninja must achieve in order to crush their enemies, see their powerful weapons and vehicles, and find out which sets each minifigure appears in.

The final part of the book features a complete list of all the LEGO NINJAGO sets for the fact-loving LEGO fans!

HISTORY OF NINJAGO ISLAND

A very long time ago, Ninjago Island was created by the First Spinjitzu Master, using the four Golden Weapons. He told his two sons— Wu and Garmadon—about the mysterious energy of these Elemental Weapons whose combined power was so great that no single person could handle them all at one time. He warned them against wicked powers that sought to control the weapons.

Upon his death, his sons swore to protect the weapons but Garmadon turned evil. He fought against Wu to gain control of the Golden Weapons, but lost and was banished to the Underworld. Wu hid the weapons in the far corners of Ninjago Island and began training some young ninja. Peace prevailed until Lord Garmadon returned and unleashed dark forces of The Cursed Realm. After Lord Garmadon's defeat at the hands of Wu's recruits, he turned wise and started helping these same ninja. But dark forces lurk in the shadows and the ninja must face many villains before peace is restored to the land...

THE OVERLORD is one of the oldest enemies of Ninjago Island. He first leads the Stone Army, and then an army of Nindroids against the ninja.

SPINJITZU

Spinjitzu is an ancient martial art, that allows any master of it to spin so quickly that they become a tornado of energy. Spinjitzu Masters usually control one of the elements. If the ninja master this skill, then they can move on to Airjitzu!

MAP OF NINJAGO ISLAND

Master Wu made a map of Ninjago Island to show the secret locations of the Elemental Weapons. The weapons now rest safely with the ninja and are used to fight villains who threaten the land.

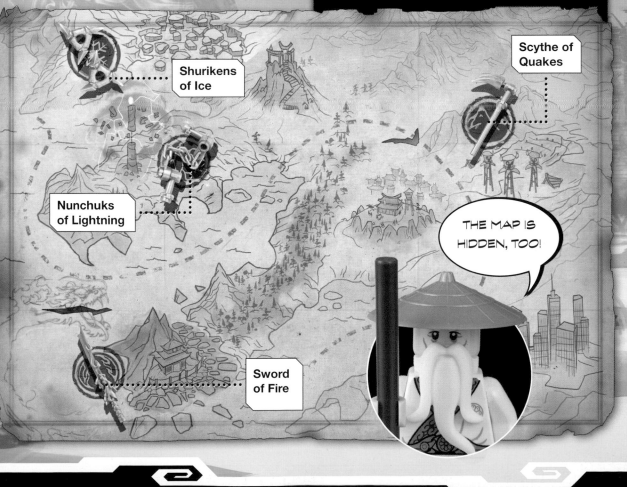

Shurikens of Ice

Scythe of Quakes

Nunchuks of Lightning

THE MAP IS HIDDEN, TOO!

Sword of Fire

THE PILOT SEASON of NINJAGO™: Masters of Spinjitzu sees the rise of Lord Garmadon. Master Wu trains four ninja to help him defeat his evil brother. However, Garmadon is not alone—he has a mighty Skeleton Army. A total of 16 awesome LEGO sets bring this season's characters, weapons, vehicles, and locations to life. Turn the page to find out more...

BANZAI! MY ICY POWER WILL SOON QUENCH YOUR FIRE, NINJA!

MASTER WU
SPINJITZU MASTER

Master Wu's beard and mustache are removable.

Magical golden writing protects Master Wu from evil.

BROTHERLY BOTHER
Master Wu and his brother, Lord
Garmadon, were trained by their
father, the First Spinjitzu Master.
He hoped that his sons would use
their skills to protect the people of
Ninjago Island. Lord Garmadon
uses his powers for evil, but Wu
carries on his father's noble legacy.

MASTER OF THE POWER of creation,
Wu is the son of the First Spinjitzu Master
who created Ninjago Island. As well
as mastering the ancient martial art of
Spinjitzu, wise Master Wu has achieved
the ultimate power. He can control all four
elements—fire, ice, lightning, and earth.

NINJA FILE

LIKES: Extreme sports
DISLIKES: Dancing
FRIENDS: Fellow ninja
FOES: Kruncha, Chopov
SKILLS: Strength
GEAR: Bow and arrow, hammer

SET NAME: Cole, Turbo Shredder, Ninja Training Outpost
SET NUMBER: 2112, 2263, 2516
YEAR: 2011

Golden emblem showing the Earth symbol

Bow and arrow for target practice

TEAM FIRST
Cole was the first student Master Wu recruited for ninja training. Cole enjoys focusing his energy and powers during Wu's grueling training routines. Target practice helps him improve his concentration and accuracy.

COLE IS AS STRONG and reliable as a rock. His natural strategic and leadership skills make him a key part of the ninja team. Cole always puts his team first and is a true friend to the other ninja. Cole can spin dirt and soil into a huge storm, reducing everything in its path to dust.

KAI

MASTER OF FIRE

Traditional head wrap made from two scarves to leave only the eyes uncovered

DID YOU KNOW?

Kai's father may have known the secrets of the ninja. He guarded a map that showed the location of four powerful weapons.

Katana sword was forged in Kai's blacksmith shop.

Sashes and belts are an essential part of a ninja's outfit.

FAMILY HISTORY

Kai and his sister, Nya, took over the Four Weapons Blacksmith Shop when their father died. Wu saw that Kai had the potential to be more than a blacksmith and trained him to use his natural "fire" to master Spinjitzu.

THIS NINJA'S ELEMENT is fire and his temper is equally hot! Kai accepts Master Wu's challenge to train as a ninja, but he must work hard to control his anger and impatience. Master Wu's faith in Kai is justified—he soon becomes a brave, loyal, and skillful ninja. He channels his fiery energy into Spinjitzu.

JAY

MASTER OF LIGHTNING

Nunchucks of Lightning are one of the four Golden Weapons.

Golden emblem on robe is the symbol for lightning.

LIGHTNING SPINJITZU

Jay was the first of the four ninja to master the art of Spinjitzu. Now, as quick as a flash, he can spin to turn into a lightning tornado crackling with electric ninja energy.

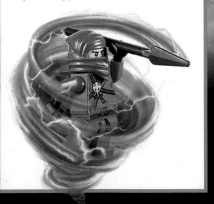

LIGHTNING IS HIS ELEMENT and Jay is lightning-fast in combat. His flair for crazy inventions, his thirst for adventure, and his sense of humor are just some of the qualities that Master Wu knew would make Jay a good, skillful ninja. Jay is also creative and loves solving problems.

ZANE
MASTER OF ICE

Zane's ninja wrap is as icy white as his element.

NINJA FILE

LIKES: Cooking
DISLIKES: Jokes
FRIENDS: Master Wu
FOES: Wyplash, Bonezai
SKILLS: Logic
GEAR: Katana sword, flat spear

SET NAME: Zane, Spinjitzu Dojo, Skull Truck, Fire Temple, Ninja Glider
SET NUMBER: 2113, 2504, 2506, 2507, 30080
YEAR: 2011

NINJA GLIDER

In Ninja Glider (set 30080), Zane has a super cool Ninja Glider made from six golden blades. Zane can silently glide up on his enemies armed with a lethal black katana.

Black hands contrast with Zane's white robes, but are featured on all the ninja recruits.

ZANE IS QUIET, serious, and focused. He learns quickly and is curious about everything. Zane watches and waits for the right moment to strike. He is so quiet and stealthy that he can creep up on his enemies without being detected. However, his friends' jokes often pass him by undetected in return!

NYA
SISTER OF KAI

Nya can use many different weapons, including daggers.

NINJA FILE

LIKES: Her independence
DISLIKES: Being kidnapped
FRIENDS: Jay
FOES: Skeleton Army
SKILLS: Tech wiz
GEAR: Daggers, staff

SET NAME: Nya, Garmadon's Dark Fortress, Fire Temple
SET NUMBER: 2172, 2505, 2507
YEAR: 2011

SECRETIVE SISTER

Nya hides her identity so that she can help the ninja, but is she also keeping secrets from them? When the Skeleton Army kidnap Nya, she soon shows the sneaky Skulkins that she has warrior skills of her own.

Red veil covers Nya's determined expression.

Robes with phoenix detail are printed on legs

DID YOU KNOW?

Nya was the first LEGO NINJAGO minifigure to have a double-sided head. She was followed by Lloyd, P.I.X.A.L., and many others.

NYA IS KAI'S younger sister. She works with Kai in the Four Weapons Blacksmith Shop. Although she isn't a ninja yet, tough Nya is determined to be better than the boys. She trains hard and, with a veil to mask her identity, she is always ready to battle evil. She uses her skills with computers to spy on their enemies.

O BECOME A
TRUE NINJA YOU MUST:

FIND AND CONTROL YOUR ELEMENT

ALWAYS BE LOYAL TO YOUR FRIENDS

LEARN TO WIELD MANY TYPES OF WEAPONS

MASTER THE ART OF STEALTH

LORD GARMADON
MASTER OF DESTRUCTION

Underworld helmet helps to control the Skeleton Army.

Thunder Bolt weapon can zap foes with electricity.

THE GREAT DEVOURER
Garmadon wasn't always bad. He was bitten by a snake called the Great Devourer as a child, and its venom made him evil. After losing a duel with Wu, Garmadon developed his evil appearance and fell into the Underworld.

MASTER WU'S EVIL brother, Lord Garmadon, is King of the Underworld. With the help of his Skeleton Army, he continues to spread fear on his dark quest to defeat his brother and the ninja, and to destroy Ninjago Island. He has trained the boneheaded Skeletons in the ways of Spinjitzu, making them fearsome opponents.

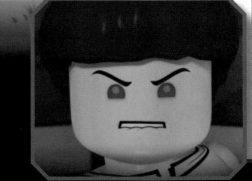

MASTER WU
DOJO LEADER

Traditional conical hat shades Wu's eyes from the sun.

Head is printed with wise eyes and gray eyebrows.

Clean white robes are Wu's training uniform.

NINJA FILE

LIKES: Riddles
DISLIKES: Sleeping ninja
FRIENDS: Ninja students
FOES: Skeleton Army
SKILLS: Endless patience
GEAR: Bo staff

SET NAME: Spinjitzu Dojo, Ninjago Battle Arena, Exclusive Weapon Training Set
SET NUMBER: 2504, 853106, 853111
YEAR: 2011

TIME FOR TEA?
Teaching four young ninja-in-training can be thirsty work! Master Wu schedules regular breaks for a refreshing cup of tea. These are often just for Wu though—the ninja must keep busy!

MASTER WU MAY BE very old, but he is an expert ninja and a fearless warrior. He plans to pass on his valuable knowledge to a new generation of ninja. Master Wu makes his students train every day, and tells them to use their brains as well as their strength. Without wisdom you can't win.

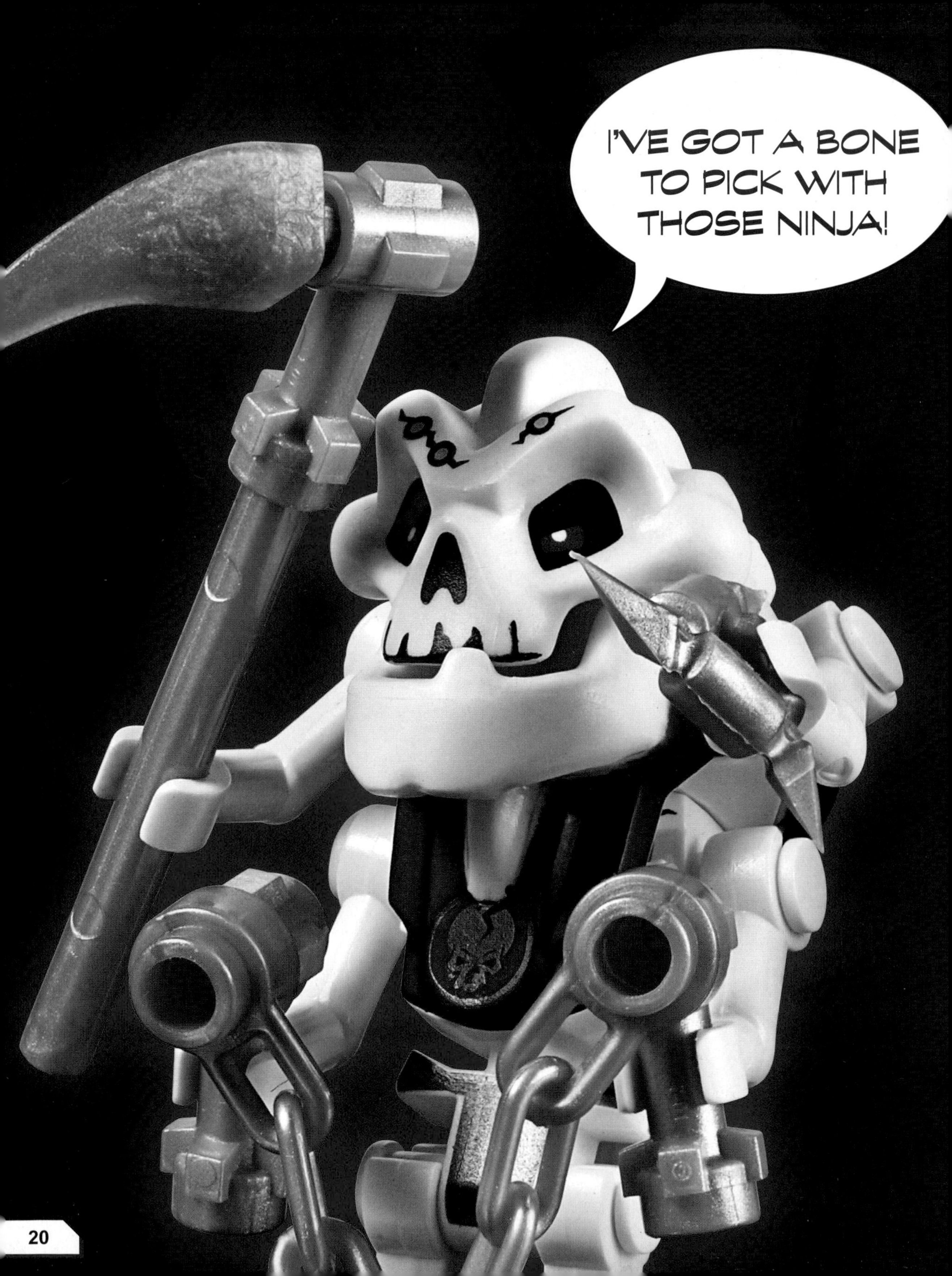
I'VE GOT A BONE TO PICK WITH THOSE NINJA!

THE BACKBONE OF THE SKELETON ARMY IS:

OBEDIENCE

ANGER

RUTHLESSNESS

EVIL

SAMUKAI
GENERAL OF FIRE

Wide, open mouth is unique in LEGO NINJAGO minifigures.

Unique skull markings

NINJA FILE

LIKES: Being in charge
DISLIKES: Following orders
FRIENDS: Fellow generals
FOES: Lord Garmadon
SKILLS: Plotting schemes
GEAR: Bone daggers

SET NAME: Garmadon's Dark Fortress, Fire Temple
SET NUMBER: 2505, 2507
YEAR: 2011

One of four bony arms allow him to wield four weapons at once

MEETING THEIR MATCH
The four trainee ninja each represent a different element, and so do their bony foes. Samukai is linked with Fire, just like Kai. Sparks fly when the pair battle, thanks to their blazing blades!

ONCE THE KING of the Underworld, Samukai's reign was overthrown by Lord Garmadon. Now, the fearsome Samukai leads the Skeleton Army in its battle against the ninja, under Garmadon's control. Garmadon plans to use four-armed Samukai to wield the four Golden Weapons.

KRUNCHA

GENERAL OF EARTH

Sophisticated Kruncha wears a monocle on his right eye.

Standard skeleton torso fits under removable armor.

Jagged golden blade is heavy and sharp.

BODY ARMOR

Kruncha's protective body armor is different to that of most other Skulkins. The shoulder pads are heavier and he doesn't wear the gray chest panel with markings on it. Only Wyplash has armor similar to Kruncha's.

LOUD, HARD, AND STRONG, Kruncha is one of the four generals in the Skeleton Army. The General of Earth, Kruncha is mean and will crush anyone who dares to get in his way. He often shouts at his foot soldiers, but is also constantly bickering with fellow general, Nuckal.

WYPLASH
GENERAL OF ICE

Shoulder pad and body protection armor

Sword with sharp curved blade

Black feet on LEGO NINJAGO skeletons differ from those on traditional LEGO skeletons.

NINJA FILE

LIKES: Keeping watch
DISLIKES: Not knowing what is going on
FRIENDS: He trusts no one
FOES: Watchful Nya
SKILLS: Stealth
GEAR: Stolen scythe blade

SET NAME: Wyplash, Skull Truck, Earth Dragon Defence
SET NUMBER: 2175, 2506, 2509
YEAR: 2011

SKULL DECORATION
Wyplash wears a bamboo hat, just like Master Wu's! Wyplash is the only Skeleton General with removable headwear. He is also the only Skeleton who has a worm crawling from the side of his skull!

Worm could be the cause of Wyplash's headaches.

WYPLASH IS A GENERAL in Garmadon's Army and Samukai's second-in-command. Stealth is his special skill, and he always watches and waits for the right moment to attack his enemy. Paranoid Wyplash can turn his huge skull backwards, which means he can always see the enemy approaching.

NUCKAL
GENERAL OF LIGHTNING

Nuckal's skull is a unique molded piece with a row of head spikes.

Metal eye patch

NINJA FILE

LIKES: Causing mayhem
DISLIKES: Being bored
FRIENDS: Skeletons of Lightning
FOES: Anyone in his way
SKILLS: Bravery
GEAR: Silver dark blade

SET NAME: Nuckal, Nuckal's ATV, Spinjitzu Dojo
SET NUMBER: 2173, 2518, 2504
YEAR: 2011

ALL-TERRAIN TERROR
Nuckal's ATV (All-Terrain Vehicle) causes destruction wherever it goes. This scary bone buggy packs a punch with its heavy armor, solid suspension, and missile launcher. It is to be avoided at all costs!

NUCKAL IS CHILDISH, wild, and very dangerous. He loves fighting, and if there is trouble to be found, Nuckal will find it! This bony brute's idea of fun is striking ninja down with his lightning-fast battle skills. His lethal moves are often combined with a cackling and electrifying laugh.

ᚠᚱᚻᚻ ᚻᚹ

SKELETON OF FIRE

DID YOU KNOW?

Despite owning a sturdy helmet, Frakjaw drives the Turbo Shredder (set 2263) wearing only a bamboo hat for protection!

NINJA FILE

LIKES: Chatting
DISLIKES: Being bored
FRIENDS: Krazi—he is the only Skeleton brave enough!
FOES: Fire Ninja Kai
SKILLS: Fearless nature
GEAR: Golden mace, dark blade, long bone

SET NAME: Skeleton Chopper, Spinjitzu Starter Set, Lightning Dragon Battle, Turbo Shredder
SET NUMBER: 30081, 2257, 2521, 2263
YEAR: 2011

Helmet with goggles protects Frakjaw in battle.

Golden mace increases Frakjaw's attack range when he launches into his Spinjitzu moves.

WEAPONS STASH

The Skeletons have a terrifying collection of weapons to use in battle. The ninja need all their skills to defeat this evil enemy. They are brutal and vicious fighters, and the legendary Frakjaw is one of the worst of all.

THIS SCARY RED-ROBED Skeleton is the toughest Skulkin in Lord Garmadon's army. He is fiery and angry and loves to fight—especially with the ninja! Frakjaw loves the sound of his own voice and sometimes it is difficult to get him to shut up. He especially likes to taunt and challenge his enemies.

26

KRAZI

SKELETON OF LIGHTNING

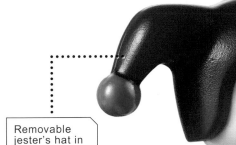

Removable jester's hat in red and blue

Red face paint completes the clownish look.

DID YOU KNOW?
It isn't only ninja that are mastering the art of Spinjitzu. Krazi's Lightning tornado is terrifying and fast!

Stolen Shuriken of Ice

POINTED PROTECTION

Krazi minifigures feature either a red and blue jester's hat or blue armor, never both. Krazi's blue shoulder spikes match those on the armor of his Lightning General, Nuckal.

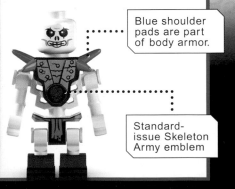

Blue shoulder pads are part of body armor.

Standard-issue Skeleton Army emblem

KRAZI BY NAME and crazy by nature, this wild menace is a Skulkin warrior in Lord Garmadon's Skeleton Army. Krazi is the fastest of the Skeletons—when he strikes he is lightning quick. Krazi's red and blue jester's hat and red face paint are signs of his crazy personality.

CHOPOV
SKELETON OF EARTH

DID YOU KNOW?

There are multiple versions of the Chopov minifigure. Other variants have a gray sash and gray shoulder spikes.

Black military helmet

Bone ax

NINJA FILE

LIKES: Dreaming big
DISLIKES: Flat tires
FRIENDS: Skeletons of Earth
FOES: Earth Ninja Cole
SKILLS: Engineering
GEAR: Bronzed bone ax

SET NAME: Chopov, Skull Motorbike, Garmadon's Dark Fortress
SET NUMBER: 2114, 2259, 2505
YEAR: 2011

Other Chopov variants have loincloth printing on the hips.

SKULL MOTORBIKE

Chopov's battle vehicle from set 2259 is a cool chopper motorbike. He uses it in battle or for quick escapes. The powerful skull hammerhead can smash anything in its path, especially ninja!

Catapult hinge mechanism

CHOPOV IS AS TOUGH as a rock. Chopov doesn't let anything get in his way, even ninja! This smart warrior is also the chief mechanic of the Skeleton Army and maintains all of the vehicles. He secretly wishes that he, instead of Bonezai, could design the Skeleton Army's super cool vehicles.

BONEZAI
SKELETON OF ICE

DID YOU KNOW?
Bonezai's name is a combination of the Japanese battle cry "banzai" and the word "bone." Creepy and cool!

NINJA FILE

LIKES: Villainous vehicles
DISLIKES: Bad drivers
FRIENDS: Chopov—or so he thinks!
FOES: Ice Ninja Zane
SKILLS: Inventing
GEAR: Silver bone ax

SET NAME: Bonezai, Ninja Ambush, Garmadon's Dark Fortress, Ninjago Battle Arena
SET NUMBER: 2115, 2258, 2505, 2520
YEAR: 2011

Don't let his smile fool you—Bonezai is a true threat!

Battle-scarred torso printing

Snowy white sash represents Bonezai's icy nature.

SNEAK ATTACK
Bonezai's head is printed with crossed eyes—perhaps as a result of a surprise blow to the head from Kai. Can Bonezai keep his cool, or will he not be able to stand the heat of Kai's attack?

BONEZAI DESIGNS all of the vehicles that the Skeleton Army use in battle. This stealthy warrior is as cold as ice and strikes a chill into the hearts of his enemies. He is so cold he can even freeze shadows! Bonezai uses his ice element abilities to win weapons and battle for glory.

KAI DX
FIRE DRAGON EXTREME

DID YOU KNOW?

Kai was the first of the ninja to find and tame his dragon. He then helped his fellow ninja do the same.

Kai's hood is unchanged from his training uniform.

Golden Fire Dragon printed on robe breathes the element of fire.

NINJA FILE

LIKES: Flying fast on Flame
DISLIKES: Losing dragon races
FRIENDS: Flame
FOES: Skeleton Army
SKILLS: Dragon-whispering
GEAR: Sword of Fire

SET NAME: Fire Temple, Mountain Shrine, Nuckal's ATV
SET NUMBER: 2507, 2254, 2518
YEAR: 2011

Kai uses a normal sword before mastering his Golden Weapon.

MASTER OF FIRE
Kai received his new ninja dragon robe after he had found his dragon and mastered the Sword of Fire. This was one of the four Golden Weapons that belonged to the First Spinjitzu Master.

KAI HAS MANAGED to tame his dragon and has gained DX (Dragon eXtreme) ranking and a new ninja dragon costume to match. Kai first enlisted the help of his dragon when the ninja needed to travel to the Underworld. Kai was able to encourage his dragon to use its incredible speed to fly to Master Wu's aid.

FIRE DRAGON
FIRE GUARDIAN

SET NAME: Fire Temple
SET NUMBER: 2507
YEAR: 2011

DID YOU KNOW?
At a certain point in their lives, the ninja's dragons must fly away and shed their scales (molt) in order to become adult dragons.

Flaming tip of tail can be used to attack enemies.

Jaws of fiery head contain a red-hot weapons launcher

THIS MIGHTY FIRE DRAGON guards the Golden Sword of Fire, which Master Wu hid in the Fire Temple. When Kai tames this dragon, he is able to control and ride him. Kai names his dragon Flame—a fitting name for a creature who is red-hot from nose to tail!

HIDDEN DRAGON
The Fire Temple set conceals the mighty Fire Dragon. Flame's wings are just visible when the temple is closed, but when open, Flame appears in all his blazing glory.

JAY DX

LIGHTNING DRAGON EXTREME

Distinctive eyebrows give Jay's identity away.

New dark blue obi sash

DRAGON CHAMPION

When the ninja aren't out fighting Skeletons, they make sure their dragons still get plenty of exercise. The ninja have regular races around the Ninjago skies. Jay loves to win—and celebrate!

JAY USED HIS INVENTING SKILLS to tame his dragon when his jokes and cooking failed to win the dragon over. He created a dragon roar amplifier to boost the volume of his dragon's battle cry. Now, with his DX ninja status and the Nunchucks of Lightning, Jay is more than ready to do battle against evil.

LIGHTNING DRAGON

LIGHTNING GUARDIAN

Two long spears mounted on the dragon's wings

Deadly flicking tail delivers a nasty shock to foes.

Claw with golden talons is attached to the dragon's wing.

FLYING FLAGS
The two flags Wisp carries feature the Japanese symbols for "dragon god." In Japan, dragons are known as "tatsu," or "ryu," and blue dragons symbolize the East of the country.

龍神

THIS LIGHTNING DRAGON guards the Golden Nunchucks of Lightning, which Master Wu hid in the desolate Floating Ruins. Jay names his dragon Wisp and once tamed, Wisp is forever loyal to Jay. Wisp shares Jay's electric powers and lightning-fast reactions.

COLE DX
EARTH DRAGON EXTREME

NINJA FILE

LIKES: Dragons (just about)
DISLIKES: Dragons (until now!)
FRIENDS: Rocky
FOES: Skeleton Army
SKILLS: Creating earthquakes
GEAR: Scythe of Quakes

SET NAME: Cole DX, Earth Dragon Defence, Ninja Battle Arena
SET NUMBER: 2170, 2509, 2520
YEAR: 2011

DID YOU KNOW?
Cole's DX ninja robes have his name and earth elemental symbol on the back. The other ninja have similar back patterns.

Scythe of Quakes is linked to the earth element.

Earth Dragon's huge scaly tail is printed on the legs.

MOVING MOTIVATION
The quickest way to Cole's heart is through his stomach, and it is the same for his dragon. Cole encourages the dragon to greater speeds by dangling a tasty roast chicken in front of his nose!

COLE HAS TO OVERCOME his biggest fear—dragons—to achieve his DX ninja status. With the courage of a true leader, Cole faces his fear and learns how to control his dragon. Against the odds, Cole becomes very fond of the beast. Next, Cole turns his attention to mastering the mighty Scythe of Quakes.

EARTH DRAGON

EARTH GUARDIAN

EARTH DRAGON

NINJA FILE

LIKES: Crushing villains
DISLIKES: Fancy flying manuevers
FRIENDS: Cole
FOES: Puny skeletons
SKILLS: Destruction
GEAR: Boulder-swinging tail

SET NAME: Earth Dragon Defence
SET NUMBER: 2509
YEAR: 2011

Flags attach to the harness Cole uses to ride Rocky.

DID YOU KNOW?

Rocky is the only Elemental Dragon with four legs and two small wings. The others have two legs and larger, clawed wings.

龍神

龍神

Powerful jaw fires stone missiles at enemies.

ARMORED BEAST

Rocky's legs and wings are protected with armored scales and he has spikes on his body. His horned head is made from a different mold to the other dragons, to match his bulky body.

THIS AWESOME Earth Dragon guards the Scythe of Quakes, which Master Wu hid in the Caves of Despair. He is the first of the Elemental Dragons that the ninja encounter in their search for the Golden Weapons. When Cole learns to control the Earth Dragon, he names him Rocky.

ZANE DX
ICE DRAGON EXTREME

Removable hood disguises Zane's face.

NINJA FILE

LIKES: Following directions
DISLIKES: Getting lost
FRIENDS: Shard
FOES: Frakjaw and friends
SKILLS: Spinjitzu skills
GEAR: Black katana sword, Shurikens of Ice

SET NAME: Zane DX, Ice Dragon Attack
SET NUMBER: 2171, 2260
YEAR: 2011

Ice Dragon breathes out freezing blasts of ice.

TAKE THE REINS
Zane has such exceptional balance that he can perch on the back of his dragon without a saddle! Zane clears some ice from the creature's back and guides him with two metal reins.

ZANE'S FIRST MEETING with his dragon didn't go very well—the beast froze Zane into a solid block of ice! As soon as he had thawed out, Zane was able to tame the dragon and earn his DX (Dragon eXtreme) ninja status. Seeing this cool couple together sends chills down the spines of their Skeleton foes.

ICE DRAGON

ICE GUARDIAN

LIKES: Cool breezes
DISLIKES: Summer
FRIENDS: Zane
FOES: Fiery Skeleton vehicles
SKILLS: Freezing enemies
GEAR: Razor-sharp claws

SET NAME: Ice Dragon Attack
SET NUMBER: 2260
YEAR: 2011

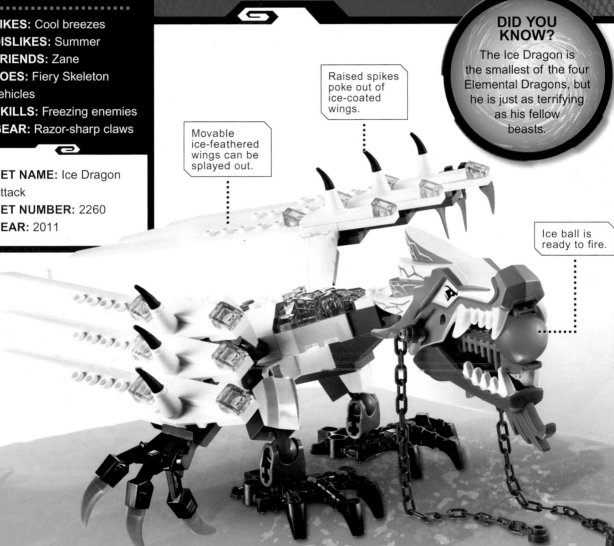

Raised spikes poke out of ice-coated wings.

Movable ice-feathered wings can be splayed out.

DID YOU KNOW?
The Ice Dragon is the smallest of the four Elemental Dragons, but he is just as terrifying as his fellow beasts.

Ice ball is ready to fire.

FRESH BREATH
Icy breath shoots out from Shard's jaws, freezing everything in its path. Solid frozen Ice balls can be fired at speed from this icy beast's terrifying jaws.

THIS ICE DRAGON guards the Golden Shurikens of Ice, which Master Wu hid inside the Ice Fortress in the Frozen Wasteland. After a frosty first encounter, Zane uses his elemental powers to find a connection with the mythical beast. He tames the dragon and names him Shard.

IN SEASON ONE of NINJAGO™: Masters of Spinjitzu a new enemy is unleashed—the venomous Serpentine. A total of 14 amazing LEGO sets bring the action to life. Turn the page and learn about all the characters—whether they have two legs or none—and meet a very special ninja...

WE WILL STOP YOU AND YOUR KIND!

MASTER WU
CAPTAIN OF DESTINY'S BOUNTY

NINJA FILE

LIKES: Meditating
DISLIKES: Being disturbed
FRIENDS: Reformed brother Garmadon
FOES: Serpentine
SKILLS: Mastery of Elements and Spinjitzu
GEAR: Bo staff

SET NAME: Destiny's Bounty
SET NUMBER: 9446
YEAR: 2012

A very similar Wu minifigure variant with a pearl-gold hat appears in Epic Dragon Battle (set 9450) and Temple of Light (set 70505).

New robes feature snake symbols to protect him from evil—and snakes!

New obi belt is a lighter color than on previous Wu minifigures.

DESTINY JET
After the snakes destroyed the ninja's old HQ, the dojo, the team found a new base in this ancient shipwreck from the desert wastelands. It hides a few surprises—such as the ability to convert it into a flying machine!

CALM AND SELF-DISCIPLINED Master Wu is the perfect teacher. He uses knowledge from years of training to teach the ninja and help them to reach the next three levels—ZX (Zen eXtreme), Kendo, and NRG. In new, lighter, robes he is on the hunt for a new base. Luckily, Cole is the only ninja who gets seasick...

COLE ZX

EARTH ZEN EXTREME

DID YOU KNOW?
The Serpentine can be controlled by sacred flute music. Zane and Cole install recordings of this music to play from the Raider, as a secret weapon!

Protective leather-style chest plate

No pauldrons appear on a variant in Car (set 30087).

This three-pronged weapon is the ultimate Serpentine repellent.

ULTRA SONIC TEAMWORK
Cole and Zane take charge of this awesome sonic vehicle, created from recycled parts. Cole drives the tank part, while Zane flies the aircraft that slots on top. With these dual modes, the Raider is the ultimate fighting machine!

THANKS TO HOURS of practice, Cole has achieved the ZX, or Zen, level of his ninja training. To mark his new status, Cole wears silver pauldrons to protect his upper body. As leader of the ninja, it is now Cole's job to help the others develop their own Zen eXtreme skills.

JAY ZX
LIGHTNING ZEN EXTREME

NINJA FILE

LIKES: The open sky
DISLIKES: Going slow
FRIENDS: ZX Ninja
FOES: Pythor
SKILLS: Piloting his jet
GEAR: Silver katanas

SET NAME: Fangpyre Truck Ambush, Ultra Sonic Raider, Epic Dragon Battle, Jay ZX, Samurai Accessory Set
SET NUMBER: 9445, 9449, 9450, 9553, 850632
YEAR: 2012, 2013

Pauldron piece has a hole at the back that can hold two katana blades.

Beneath his hood, Jay wears the same steely expression as on his original minifigure (p.13).

New robes feature one arm covered in protective silver armor.

ZX ROBES
Jay's new robes help him to be more agile. The light armor is flexible, and without his pauldrons, as in sets 9442 and 30085, he fits snugly into his Storm Fighter, ready to blast through the skies.

DID YOU KNOW?
Jay loves flying his Storm Fighter (set 9442). He is super fast in combat in the ground and in the sky. Jay's enemies are often caught by surprise.

JAY HAS LEARNT many new skills from his teacher, Master Wu. His dedication to learning the ancient martial arts has certainly earned Jay his ZX ninja status. With his new skills, Jay is faster than ever in combat. The enemy won't see Jay's silver blade coming (or the dagger hidden in his robes)!

KAI ZX
FIRE ZEN EXTREME

Removable ZX
crown and
hood with new
gold detail

Throwing
stars tucked
into belt

Protective
chest plate
worn over
red tunic

SURPRISE WEAPON
In Rattlecopter (set 9443), a Kai
ZX variant comes equipped with a
unique extra weapon—a jet pack!
This useful contraption fits onto a
bracket on Kai's back, allowing
him to launch a surprise attack
over his enemies from above.

Air-resistant
adjuster panels

SINCE BATTLING the Skeleton Army, Kai
has worked hard to achieve the next level of
his ninja training. His ZX minifigure is ready
to take on new challenges and enemies.
His robes are printed with protective armor,
weapons, and two red belts that secure
everything in place during battle.

ZANE ZX
ICE ZEN EXTREME

In Hidden Sword (set 30086) a variant of this minifigure appears without golden armor.

NINJA FILE

LIKES: Taboganning
DISLIKES: Emotions
FRIENDS: Dr. Julien
FOES: Pythor
SKILLS: Piloting the flying Ultra Sonic Raider
GEAR: Shurikens of Ice

SET NAME: Venomari Shrine, Fangpyre Truck Ambush, Ultra Sonic Raider, Zane ZX, Samurai Accessory Set
SET NUMBER: 9440, 9445, 9449, 9554, 850632
YEAR: 2012

DID YOU KNOW?
Zane's creator, Dr. Julien, turned Zane's memory switch off, so Zane wouldn't know he was a Nindroid and could live a normal life.

Zane's new robes feature entwined rope belts and a plain white undershirt.

ICE MASTER
The Golden Shurikens of Ice are Zane's preferred weapon. The ZX warrior has perfected his aim with these lethal spinning stars and can even throw them while speeding along on his open-topped snowmobile in set 9445!

Robe edging and armor belt clip printed on legs.

STEALTHY ZANE IS NOW an expert ZX, or Zen eXtreme, ninja. His ZX minifigure features gold pauldrons and gold detailing on his hood. Thanks to the new outfit he can carry two swords on his back, so he can fight more than one Serpent at once! Zane's mastery of the element of ice has also reached an even higher level.

NINJA FILE

LIKES: Sword practice
DISLIKES: Being told to stay away from fighting, not being taken seriously
FRIENDS: Jay
FOES: Serpentine
SKILLS: Building robots
GEAR: Giant mech sword

SET NAME: Samurai Mech, Samurai X
SET NUMBER: 9448, 9566
YEAR: 2012

ROBOT WARS

The Samurai Mech is a massive robot controlled by Samurai X. It comes equipped with a fierce arsenal of weapons—including a cannon shooter, missiles, sharp claws for crushing, and a mighty sword—but will all this be enough to fend off the Serpents?

Ornamental spiked Samurai crest tops protective helmet.

Red mask hides Nya's face and true identity.

Nya has already found one of the venomous Fang blades!

Protective body armor covers red warrior dress robes and comes with extended shoulder pads.

Samurai helmet conceals Nya in the cockpit.

DID YOU KNOW?
Smart Nya is able to cure a Fangpyre bite and knows that getting just one Fang Blade will stop the Great Devourer!

WHO IS HIDING behind Samurai X's mask? For a while no one knows who this warrior is, but one day the truth is revealed to Jay. Samurai X is Nya, Kai's sister! The ninja are surprised, but soon see that Nya is just as skilled as they are. She might even be able to teach them some things.

LLOYD GARMADON

SON OF LORD GARMADON

NINJA FILE

LIKES: Causing trouble
DISLIKES: Being left out
FRIENDS: Serpentine
FOES: The ninja
SKILLS: Annoying everyone nearby
GEAR: Lightning dagger and golden Constrictai Staff

SET NAME: Lloyd Garmadon, Rattlecopter, Fangpyre Wrecking Ball
SET NUMBER: 9552, 9443, 9457
YEAR: 2012

Black-hooded cloak is removable.

Golden Constrictai Staff has great power, which makes Lloyd a little wary of it!

TWO-FACED

Having the most evil father in all the land is a difficult legacy for Lloyd to live up to. He switches between playing annoying pranks and being scared of his father's powers—as his face reflects!

Green "5" hints at Lloyd's future as the fifth ninja.

LLOYD GARMADON is not as bad as his father, Lord Garmadon. He attends Darkley's Boarding School for Bad Boys and is more interested in candy and practical jokes than plotting to take over Ninjago Island. Young Lloyd accidentally releases the Serpentine tribes and becomes their unlikely leader.

GREEN NINJA
MASTER OF ALL ELEMENTS

Pale shirt worn beneath special Green Ninja robes.

Detachable protective shoulder and back armor

NINJA FILE

LIKES: Becoming a hero

DISLIKES: Fighting his father

FRIENDS: The ninja

FOES: Forces of evil!

SKILLS: Wielding the powers of the four elements

GEAR: Golden katana

SET NAME: Epic Dragon Battle, Lloyd ZX

SET NUMBER: 9450, 9547

YEAR: 2012

Silver detailing on robes and belt clasp

KIMONO KEEPSAKE

A variant of the Green Ninja was available exclusively in the original DK LEGO NINJAGO *Character Encyclopedia*. This minifigure had an elaborate, green-and-gold kimono, perhaps hinting at a golden future for Lloyd.

AN ANCIENT PROPHECY foretold that a Green Ninja would rise above all others, to fight the darkness. Surprisingly, the Green Ninja's identity is revealed to be none other than Lloyd Garmadon. The transformative powers of the Golden Weapons turned him into the Green Ninja.

KENDO COLE

MARTIAL ARTS MASTER

NINJA FILE

LIKES: Dodging danger
DISLIKES: Snake attacks
FRIENDS: Master Wu
FOES: Fangpyre Tribe
SKILLS: His earth tornado
GEAR: Golden double-bladed ax, scythe

SET NAME: Fangpyre Mech, Fangpyre Wrecking Ball, Kendo Cole
SET NUMBER: 9455, 9457, 9551
YEAR: 2012

Helmet similar to those worn by LEGO® American Football players.

Cole's Kendo body armour is bulkier than the other ninja's.

Black is always in fashion!

WRECKING BALL

Cole's heavy-duty Kendo armour is really put to the test when he takes on the Fangpyre Wrecking Ball. This articulated crane is driven by Fangdam, who wants to crush the Ninja of Earth beneath his heavy, spiked wrecking ball!

DID YOU KNOW?

Kendo Cole appears in a total of three sets—one more than all the other Kendo ninja variants.

THE NINJA ARE always ready to learn new skills to give them an edge over their enemies. When Master Wu teaches them the complex martial art called Kendo, they have to train very hard to master this Samurai style of fighting. As Kendo can be dangerous, Cole wears a protective helmet, mask, and body armor.

KENDO KAI
ARMORED ATTACK

NINJA FILE
....

LIKES: Winning
DISLIKES: Heavy armor
FRIENDS: Kendo Ninja
FOES: Rattla
SKILLS: Advanced
Spinjitzu plus swordplay
GEAR: Sword of Fire

SET NAME: Spinner Battle
Arena, Training Set
SET NUMBER: 9456, 9558
YEAR: 2012

Kai's red neck scarf can be seen through a gap in his armor.

Grills protect Kai's face, but still allow him to see clearly.

SWORD OF FIRE
Sword-fighting is an important part of Kendo. Fortunately, Kai is already an expert with his elemental weapon, the Sword of Fire. Kendo is no problem for Kai, and he uses it to take on Rattla in the snake arena!

Thinner, lighter breastplate is more practical for fast, spinning moves.

TO BE KENDO NINJA, all four must reach a higher level of physical agility and mental control. With his new armor and helmet, this variant of Kai is all set to take on the physical knocks and blows of Kendo. However, he will need to practice remaining calm before he can achieve this new level.

KENDO ZANE

READY FOR ANYTHING

Helmet is specially designed to protect the neck as well as the head.

NINJA FILE

LIKES: Winter sports
DISLIKES: Shipwrecks
FRIENDS: Jay, Master Wu
FOES: Skales, Slithraa
SKILLS: Balancing tricks
GEAR: Silver sai, golden mace, katana

SET NAME: Destiny's Bounty, Kendo Zane
SET NUMBER: 9446, 9563
YEAR: 2012

Simple silver sai for close-range fights

Belt fastens round waist, with tie printing continuing on legs.

MULTITASKING
To master Kendo combined with Spinjitzu while also holding this long golden mace, Zane must have excellent balance.

ZANE IS THE MASTER OF ICE, but in his Kendo outfit he looks more like an ice hockey player! Zane just thinks he looks cool, and is more than ready to take on the Serpentine who are attacking their ninja base—the *Destiny's Bounty*. Zane's armor is lightweight, so he won't sink if he falls overboard!

KENDO JAY

SHIPSHAPE AND SEAWORTHY

NINJA FILE

LIKES: Boats, dancing
DISLIKES: Being grounded
FRIENDS: Lloyd, possibly
FOES: Skales, Slithraa
SKILLS: Flying the jet part of the *Destiny's Bounty*
GEAR: Dark talons, golden blade, katana

SET NAME: Destiny's Bounty, Kendo Jay Booster Pack
SET NUMBER: 9446, 5000030
YEAR: 2012

DID YOU KNOW?
Kendo fighters use bamboo swords called "shinai" for training. Now an expert, Jay has graduated to a golden blade.

Shoulder pads are grooved and extra-tough.

Golden blade slices through the air as Jay flies in a lightning Spinjitzu tornado!

KENDO HQ
The ninja have plenty of room to practice Kendo on their secret headquarters—the *Destiny's Bounty*. However, when their base comes under Serpentine attack, the ninja have to quickly put their Kendo skills to the test.

ONCE THEY HAVE MASTERED Kendo, the ninja can use any weapons they like. Jay chooses the dark talons and a golden blade as the perfect accessories for his lightning-fast abilities. This new armor doesn't appear to be slowing Jay down at all!

PYTHOR P. CHUMSWORTH

LAST OF THE ANACONDRAI

NINJA FILE

LIKES: Evil schemes
DISLIKES: Getting his hands dirty
FRIENDS: Serpentine minions
FOES: Everyone!
SKILLS: Evil mastermind
GEAR: Fang Blades

SET NAME: Ultra Sonic Raider
SET NUMBER: 9449
YEAR: 2012

Long necks are the Anacondrai's most distinctive feature.

Open-mouthed head with fangs for eating friends and foes alike!

Fangpyre Fang Blade is already in Pythor's possession.

DID YOU KNOW?

While imprisoned, the Anacondrai started eating each other! Pythor ended up a general with no followers, but a full stomach!

NEVER TRUST A SNAKE

When Pythor finally gets his hands on all four Fang Blades, he uses them to release the Great Devourer. His moment of triumph is short-lived—the first thing the Great Devourer does is devour Pythor!

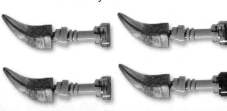

PYTHOR WAS GENERAL of the villainous Anacondrai, the strongest and most feared snake tribe around. After their capture and imprisonment many years ago, he is now the tribe's last surviving member. Pythor wants all four Fang Blades so that he can release the Great Devourer and destroy Ninjago Island.

LORD GARMADON
FOUR-ARMED FOE

Removable second torso with two extra arms

NINJA FILE

LIKES: Eating Condensed Evil

DISLIKES: Teamwork

FRIENDS: None

FOES: Great Devourer

SKILLS: Combat skills

GEAR: Golden Weapons

SET NAME: Epic Dragon Battle, Destiny's Bounty

SET NUMBER: 9450, 9446

YEAR: 2012

Silver torso printing can be seen under the second torso.

DID YOU KNOW?

This version of Lord Garmadon is made up of the same head and body as his 2011 minifigure, with an extra upper body piece.

FACING AN OLD FOE

With his extra arms, Garmadon is the only person able to wield all four Golden Weapons. This surprising ally lends the ninja his many hands in a battle against the Great Devourer—the snake whose bite turned him evil.

HE'S BACK! Having returned from the Underworld, Lord Garmadon still wants to take over Ninjago Island, and also wants revenge on the ninja for thwarting his evil plans. This time he is stronger than ever, with a double torso and four arms! However, his love for his son might just be even stronger.

THE GREAT DEVOURER
KING OF THE SNAKES

NINJA FILE

LIKES: Eating
DISLIKES: Indigestion
FRIENDS: Serpentine tribes
FOES: Ninja
SKILLS: Eating
GEAR: Super-strong jaws

SET NAME: Epic Dragon Battle
SET NUMBER: 9450
YEAR: 2012

DID YOU KNOW?
Legend has it that the four Fang Blades were created from discarded teeth of the Great Devourer.

LEGO blade pieces make sharp snake fangs.

Printed curved pieces are used to create tough scaly body.

Giant mouth consumes everything it finds.

The Great Devourer's tail is posable.

A BITE TO EAT
Watch out, ninja! The Great Devourer's fang-filled mouth is big enough to hold a minifigure—before crushing and eating it! Let's hope the other ninja come to Jay's rescue in a flash!

THE GREAT DEVOURER was kept safely imprisoned away from Ninjago Island's citizens for many years. Now, Pythor has released the beast from the Lost City of Ouroboros, causing chaos. The giant snake will consume all of Ninjago Island in its terrifying jaws if it is not stopped.

ULTRA DRAGON

FOUR HEADS ARE BETTER THAN ONE

NINJA FILE

LIKES: Independence
DISLIKES: Being controlled for too long
FRIENDS: Green Ninja
FOES: Great Devourer
SKILLS: Firing four missiles at once
GEAR: Four heads, tail

SET NAME: Epic Dragon Battle
SET NUMBER: 9450
YEAR: 2012

DID YOU KNOW?
The Ultra Dragon's four heads come from the Lightning Dragon, the Earth Dragon, the Fire Dragon, and the Ice Dragon.

Handle moves wings up and down

Protective shield is a conical hat piece.

ULTRA RIDER
As the Green Ninja, Lloyd rides the Ultra Dragon to join the battle with the slippery Great Devourer. The ninja use the dragon to distract the snake so that Lord Garmadon can strike the final blow!

THE ULTRA DRAGON is formed from the four Elemental Dragons after they migrate to shed their scales. They return metamorphosed into one mighty, four-headed dragon! This huge creature can flap its wings and flick its tail, and is controlled by the Green Ninja, who rides on its back.

O SLITHER LIKE A SERPENTINE YOU MUST:

MASTER YOUR TRIBE'S SPECIAL POWER

BE VICIOUS, CUNNING, AND SNEAKY

KEEP YOUR FANGS SHARPENED

ALWAYS OBEY YOUR GENERAL

ACIDICUS
VENOMARI GENERAL

DID YOU KNOW?

The Venomari tribe's toxic venom causes terrible hallucinations in its victims. Acidicus keeps a vial of anti-venom in a special staff.

Acidicus has two side fangs as well as two front fangs.

NINJA FILE

LIKES: Devious weapons

DISLIKES: Venom shortages

FRIENDS: Other generals

FOES: Skalidor, at times

SKILLS: Inventive mind

GEAR: Venomari Fang Blade

SET NAME: Epic Dragon Battle

SET NUMBER: 9450

YEAR: 2012

All Serpent Generals have a snake tail instead of legs.

ONE OF FOUR

There are four ancient silver Fang Blades, one for each of the four large tribes. Each blade is filled with the venom of its tribe. The Venomari blade has a gruesome green vial of venom at its base.

GENERAL OF THE Venomari Army, Acidicus is very crafty. He has constructed special vials that the Venomari use to carry extra venom in their combat gear, so they never run out of poison in battle. How brilliantly evil! However, no one knows where clever Acidicus keeps his own vials—maybe there are pockets in his tail!

LIZARU

VENOMARI WARRIOR

Two sinister yellow eyes on each side of face

Distinctive striped head markings

DID YOU KNOW?
Head shape and printing gives important clues to a Serpent's rank in their tribe. Lizaru's seniority is reflected in his head spikes.

Scaly, scarred torso similar to other members of the Venomari tribe

NO SWAMP LIKE HOME
It isn't just the Venomari's spray that is toxic—their Ninjago swamp homes are, too! The swamps are so dangerous that the ninja are knocked out when they visit.

THIS FOUR-FANGED warrior is second-in-command to Acidicus. Lizaru runs a potion-making business, concocting lethal venoms for other Serpents. But when he isn't cooking up poisons, he is cooking up trouble! Lizaru gets so focused on his plotting, he often goes weeks without food.

SPITTA
VENOMARI WARRIOR

Green coloring with red detail is common for Venomari soldiers.

Silver battle mace is not filled with venom, but it can still leave a sting!

VENOM SUPPLIER
Spitta uses the vials invented by Acidicus to store his excess venom. He sells it to the other snakes in his tribe, for times when they can't produce enough venom of their own. They carry specially adapted weapons into battle, with venom vials attached.

THIS VENOMARI WARRIOR'S name is no mystery! Spitta's fangs are so large that his mouth is permanently open. Because of this, he drools a lot, leaking venom wherever he goes. Yuck—how slimy! Fortunately for Spitta, this means he is always stocked up with venom for battle.

LASHA
VENOMARI SCOUT

DID YOU KNOW?
Lasha's minifigure wears the same cobra headpiee as Rattla (p.69), although Lasha's is lime green and Rattla's is gray, with different decorations.

Missing eye was lost in battle.

Bandolier shoulder belt to hold vials

NINJA FILE

LIKES: Playing "I spy"
DISLIKES: Sweet treats
FRIENDS: Fellow scout—Rattla
FOES: Watchful Zane
SKILLS: Stealth
GEAR: Stolen scythe blade

SET NAME: Lasha, Lasha's Bite Cycle
SET NUMBER: 9562, 9447
YEAR: 2012

BITE CYCLE
Sneaky Lasha is perfectly equipped for his role as a Venomari scout. He speeds about on his fearsome Bite Cycle looking out for enemies and gathering information for his leaders.

LASHA IS THE BEST scout in his tribe, even though he has lost an eye. He keeps a lookout for enemies and prey for the Venomari to attack. His fangs aren't as useful as his eyes, though. They are too small to produce much venom and they often hurt because he ate too much candy when he was a young Serpent.

FANGTOM
FANGPYRE GENERAL

Two small heads sprouting from original neck

Like all the Serpent Generals, Fangtom has a tail instead of legs.

CAN'T GET THE STAFF
As General of the Fangpyre tribe, Fangtom carries the Golden Fangpyre Staff. A vial of anti-venom tailored to the Fangpyre's unique poison is held in the staff, and its end is twisted like a serpent's tail.

FANGTOM IS THE Fangpyre tribe's general. He accidentally bit himself when he was trying to turn one of his victims into a snake and his poison caused his head to form two smaller heads. Two heads are definitely better than one for Fangtom. He is the brains of the tribe and can cause double the trouble for the ninja!

NINJA FILE

LIKES: Beating ninja
DISLIKES: Not having his ideas listened to
FRIENDS: Fangtom
FOES: Ninja pests
SKILLS: Brotherly support
GEAR: Viper sidekick

SET NAME: Fangdam, Fangpyre Wrecking Ball, Fangpyre Truck Ambush
SET NUMBER: 9571, 9457, 9445
YEAR: 2012

Double-headed head piece is identical to that of his brother, Fangtom.

Fangpyre scale pattern continues onto legs.

White arms on red body are a reverse of Fang-Suei, who has red arms and a white body.

FANGPYRE TRUCK

Fast and ferocious, Fangdam has a need for speed! He has used his venom to upgrade a truck with new snake-like features. The Fangpyre Truck's giant snake head has opening and closing jaws to snap up ninja.

FANGDAM IS A WARRIOR and second-in-command of the Fangpyre tribe. Fellow Serpent Fang-Suei once mistook him for a desert slug and bit him. The bite made him grow another head. That isn't Fangdam's only likeness with his general, Fangtom—the two Serpents are brothers!

FANG-SUEI

FANGPYRE SOLDIER

Distinctive narrow head and long neck is the same mold as that used for Chokun (p.72), but here in Fangpyre colors.

(p.72)

DID YOU KNOW?

The Fangpyre are viper-like snakes. A poisonous bite from a Fangpyre can turn anything or anyone into a snake.

NINJA FILE

LIKES: Fruit

DISLIKES: Desert heat

FRIENDS: Fangpyres—before he bit them!

FOES: Ninja

SKILLS: Driving the Fangpyre Mech and piloting the Rattlecopter

GEAR: Banana weapons

SET NAME: Rattlecopter, Fangpyre Mech, Fang-Suei

SET NUMBER: 9443, 9455, 9567

YEAR: 2012

Unique necklace made of fangs

MECH MENACE

The Fangpyre Mech is Fang-Suei's battle robot. This massive mechanical monster is armed with fangs, grabbing hands and a poison missile launcher—all under Fang-Suei's complete control.

FEARSOME FANG-SUEI is the strongest of the Fangpyre tribe soldiers and is quick to act on orders. He is always hungry and if he hasn't eaten, anyone who gets in his way is likely to become a tasty snack! He can turn people and machines into snakes with one deadly bite of his extra large fangs.

SNAPPA
FANGPYRE SCOUT

Viper-like headpiece fits onto a regular minifigure head.

Snappa wears a similar fanged necklace to Fang-Suei, but with fewer teeth attached.

NINJA FILE

LIKES: Shouting
DISLIKES: Staying calm
FRIENDS: No one
FOES: Jay
SKILLS: Fighting with multiple weapons at once
GEAR: Temporarily, the Fangpyre Staff

SET NAME: Jay's Storm Fighter, Snappa
SET NUMBER: 9442, 9564
YEAR: 2012

Unusual all-white body

FIGHTING LIGHTNING
In set 9442, Snappa has taken the Fangpyre Staff, with its powerful anti-venom, to the snakes' mountain-top shrine. Jay wants it back. However, Snappa will not surrender it without a fight.

SNAPPY SNAPPA is famous for his quick temper. He is a Fangpyre Scout, and is not very popular. His hot temper and lack of brain power makes it hard for others to like him. He usually bites first and worries about the consequences later. Of course, by then it is usually too late for his victims...

SKALES

HYPNOBRAI GENERAL

Blue cobra-like hood with hypnotic pattern.

Battle pike can grab and snap other weapons.

NINJA FILE

LIKES: Seizing control
DISLIKES: Incompetent leaders
FRIENDS: Fangpyre General Fangtom
FOES: Slithraa, ninja
SKILLS: Fang-Kwon-Do
GEAR: Pike, Golden Staff

SET NAME: Cole's Tread Assault, Destiny's Bounty
SET NUMBER: 9444, 9446
YEAR: 2012

DID YOU KNOW?

There is no love lost between the Serpentine tribes, but at one time, the Hypnobrai and Fangpyre tribes were allies.

HYPNOTIC!

Now that he is General of the Hypnobrai Tribe, Skales looks after the Hypnobrai Golden Staff. As the Hypnobrai have powerful, hypnotic eyes, this Staff contains the anti-venom to reverse a hypnotic trance.

THIS COLD AND CALCULATING snake became leader of the Hypnobrai tribe when he beat General Slithraa in a fight. Skales is one of the toughest Serpents around, and is always looking for opportunities to fulfull his ambitions for control and power. He is skilled in Fang-Kwon-Do, an ancient martial art.

SLITHRAA
EX-HYPNOBRAI GENERAL

Without the Golden Staff, Slithraa must content himself with simpler blades.

NINJA FILE

LIKES: A simple life

DISLIKES: Uprisings

FRIENDS: Lloyd Garmadon

FOES: Skales

SKILLS: Giving orders that are never listened to

GEAR: Fang blades

SET NAME: Destiny's Bounty, Slithraa

SET NUMBER: 9446, 9573

YEAR: 2012

DON'T LOOK NOW

Slithraa was the victim of his own hypnosis skills when he attempted to hypnotize Lloyd Garmadon—and his gaze hit a reflective ice surface and backfired on himself! From that moment Slithraa was under the control of juvenile Lloyd, to the displeasure of the tribe.

Swirling blue and yellow Hypnobrai patterns decorate torso, head, and legs.

AFTER HIS HUMILIATING DEFEAT at the hands of his second-in-command, Skales, Slithraa lost his tail and his position as general, and grew legs again. Meanwhile, Skales grew a tail and took Slithraa's place as leader! Demoted to a warrior, Slithraa was forced to swear loyalty to Skales.

MEZMO
HYPNOBRAI SOLDIER

NINJA FILE

LIKES: Being his own boss
DISLIKES: Being told what to do by Lloyd Garmadon
FRIENDS: Ambitious Skales
FOES: Lloyd Garmadon
SKILLS: Powerful hypnosis
GEAR: Golden Double Ax

SET NAME: Mezmo
SET NUMBER: 9555
YEAR: 2012

Two large fangs overhang Mezmo's mouth.

Blue, yellow, and gray coloring matches the other members of his tribe.

DID YOU KNOW?
Mezmo feels he deserves more power in his tribe and wants to be promoted to a higher rank.

FANG-TASTIC
When Mezmo wants something, he sets out to get it. In his one-set appearance, he wields a variety of weapons. Mezmo wants his noble tribe to be free from the control of Lloyd Garmadon, and he thinks fanged axes like this Golden Double Ax will do the job.

MEZMO BY NAME, mesmerizing by nature—just don't look into this snake's swirly red eyes! Like all Hypnobrai, Mezmo can hypnotize his enemies into doing whatever he wants. He is a smart and confident soldier in the Hypnobrai tribe and if he doesn't agree with orders, he won't follow them.

RATTLA
HYPNOBRAI SCOUT

NINJA FILE
....

LIKES: Singing (badly)
DISLIKES: Practicing hypnosis
FRIENDS: Fellow Hypnobrai Scouts
FOES: Kai and the ninja
SKILLS: Spinjitzu
GEAR: Spear, golden dark blade

SET NAME: Kai's Blade Cycle, Spinner Battle Arena, Starter Set, Rattla
SET NUMBER: 9441, 9456, 9579, 30088
YEAR: 2012

Powerful red-eyed hypnotic stare

Each of the Hypnobrai have unique markings beginning at the very top of their heads.

With a weapon in his hand, Rattla is a very powerful fighter.

IN THE SNAKE ARENA
In set 9456, Kendo Kai and Rattla battle it out one-on-one. There is a weapon rack on the back wall and the two warriors can choose to use any of the seven weapons clipped in place. Rattla thinks his blade will give him the edge.

Rattla's Spinjitzu spinner comes with purple snake head adornments and Hypnobrai markings.

AS THE SCOUT for the Hypnobrai Army, Rattla is at the bottom of the chain. He is not known for his brains, but he is loyal and follows orders. As his hypnotic powers are not very strong, he experiments with different techniques to confuse his enemies—such as singing or talking them to sleep with stories!

SKALIDOR

CONSTRICTAI GENERAL

NINJA FILE

LIKES: Lounging about
DISLIKES: Moving fast
FRIENDS: General Acidicus
FOES: The Ultra Dragon
SKILLS: Sitting on enemies
GEAR: Double-bladed battle ax

SET NAME: Epic Dragon Battle
SET NUMBER: 9450
YEAR: 2012

The general wears a distinctive headpiece with silver spikes.

DID YOU KNOW?
The Constrictai Serpents live underground in caves and tunnels. When they move above ground they are so heavy that they make cracks in the earth.

This weapon is multifunctional—pairing a sharp spear with a double-headed ax.

BATTLE HUNGRY
Alongside General Acidicus of the Venomari tribe, Skalidor leads the epic battle of good versus evil as the ninja, and the Ultra Dragon, take on the Serpentine and the Great Devourer. The snakes want to devour all of Ninjago Island in their hungry jaws!

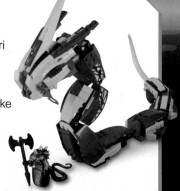

PLUMP BUT POWERFUL Skalidor is General of the Constrictai tribe. He isn't quite as athletic as the rest of his tribe but he can can crush his enemy with a single blow, or even with the weight of his body. Ninja, don't be fooled by his size—Skalidor's reflexes are fast!

BYTAR
CONSTRICTAI WARRIOR

Left eye is scarred from battle.

NINJA FILE

LIKES: Eating, fighting, sleeping
DISLIKES: Baths
FRIENDS: Snike
FOES: Samurai X, aka Nya
SKILLS: Crushing enemies
GEAR: Silver battle mace

SET NAME: Samurai Mech, Bytar
SET NUMBER: 9448, 9556
YEAR: 2012

Bytar's headpiece is from a different mold to General Skalidor's, and features bright orange spikes.

CATAPULT AMBUSH
Bytar teams up with scout Snike to fight Nya in her Samurai Mech. Using a customized catapult, they can launch missiles—or even themselves—towards Samurai X. This mechanism certainly helps them to reach heights that their legs cannot!

All the Constrictai have short, stumpy legs.

THIS MUSCLE-BOUND warrior is second-in-command in the Constrictai tribe. Bytar is a bully who likes to work out when he isn't fighting. Unfortunately, he doesn't like to wash, so he does not smell good! Stinky, brutish Bytar eats and beats anything within reach.

CHOKUN
CONSTRICTAI SOLDIER

Sinister, narrow head with gray and white scales

NINJA FILE

LIKES: Singing in Pythor's band—the "Treble Makers"
DISLIKES: Thinking hard
FRIENDS: General Skalidor
FOES: Master Wu, Ultra Dragon
SKILLS: Biting, fighting
GEAR: Golden mace

SET NAME: Epic Dragon Battle, Weapon Pack
SET NUMBER: 9450, 9591
YEAR: 2012

The Constrictai soldiers and scouts have similar orange torsos, but unique grey scale markings.

SNAKE PRISON
When the snakes manage to lock Master Wu in their Underworld Serpentine jail, Chokun is put on guard duty. The prison has front and back doors, both of which can be opened, so Chokun must stay on high alert to enure his charge does not escape!

DON'T BE FOOLED by this snake's small head—Chokun has huge, sharp fangs and a killer bite! All the Constrictai are short in stature, but what Chokun lacks in height and muscle, he makes up for in soldiering skills. Chokun is a soldier and forms the front-line defence for the Constrictai tribe.

SNIKE
CONSTRICTAI SCOUT

NINJA FILE

LIKES: Finding weapons
DISLIKES: Target practice
FRIENDS: Bytar
FOES: Nya
SKILLS: Keen eyesight
GEAR: Fang Blade

SET NAME: Samurai Mech
SET NUMBER: 9448
YEAR: 2012

Separate headpiece with boa attachment slots on top of minifigure head.

DID YOU KNOW?
Rare Snike is the only Serpentine Scout to have short legs. His minifigure only appears in one set and he does not have his own spinner.

While Chokun has gray arms, Snike's are orange.

All-orange attire probably goes unnoticed by color-blind Snike!

HIDE AND SNEAK
Snike proves his worth as a scout when he helps Pythor get hold of the second of the four Fang Blades needed to release the Great Devourer.

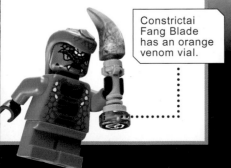

Constrictai Fang Blade has an orange venom vial.

SHORT-LEGGED SNIKE is a scout and a sniper in the Constrictai tribe. He is dedicated to his job, but as well as being color-blind, he is slightly cross-eyed and he doesn't always hit his targets at the first attempt. Despite this, Snike is big in confidence and thinks he is a skilled sniper.

HOW TO
MASTER YOUR DRAGON:

UNLOCK YOUR TRUE POTENTIAL

CAREFULLY APPROACH THE DRAGON

MAINTAIN STEADY EYE-CONTACT

USE SPINJITZU TO MOUNT THE DRAGON

NRG ZANE

ICY BLAST

NINJA FILE

LIKES: Icy cold colors
DISLIKES: The color pink
FRIENDS: NRG ninja
FOES: His own memories
SKILLS: Complete mastery of ice
GEAR: Elemental power

SET NAME: NRG Zane
SET NUMBER: 9590
YEAR: 2012

Sharp, jagged burst on Zane's chest resembles a powerful blast of ice energy.

Zane is the only NRG ninja to have hands in a different color to his arms.

SECRET PAST
Uncovering his real memories is quite overwhelming for Zane. It takes him some time to adjust to the truth—that he is, in fact, a Nindroid and therefore very different to his ninja friends.

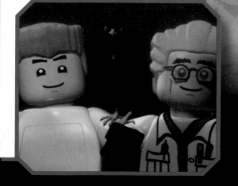

ZANE HAS HAD MANY challenges to deal with, but he is the first of the ninja to realize his full potential. For him, it means learning that he is really a robot—after discovering his memory switch and restoring his memories of Dr. Julien. Having accepted the truth in his heart, Zane is more determined than ever to stop the snakes.

NRG JAY
BOLT FROM THE BLUE

Ninja hood is no longer a plain blue, but decorated.

Lightning energy crackles around Jay's eyes.

Jay's NRG outfit features an eye-catching new lightning design emblazoned on his chest.

DID YOU KNOW?
There are still more levels of training to follow NRG status. As well as Spinjitzu, the ninja will go on to learn Airjitzu!

CATALYST
Nya uses her healing skills to heal Jay from his snake-induced injury. By healing him with a kiss, Jay must confront his true feelings—and free both himself and Nya from a snake trap—before unlocking his true potential.

JAY HAS LONG hidden a secret crush on Nya. But it is these feelings that help him to reach his full potential. When he cuts himself on a Fangpyre fossil skeleton and starts to turn into a snake, a kiss from Nya cures him and allows him to achieve his full NRG ninja status.

NRG COLE
SOLID AS A ROCK

NINJA FILE

LIKES: Being in control
DISLIKES: Not progressing
FRIENDS: NRG ninja
FOES: His history with his father
SKILLS: Complete mastery of earth
GEAR: Elemental power

SET NAME: NRG Cole
SET NUMBER: 9572
YEAR: 2012

DID YOU KNOW?
Each of the NRG ninja variants appears in one set only, making their true potential the rarest level of all!

Earth emblem appears in nuclear-bright colors on Cole's new robes.

Cole's favorite color is actually orange, but his new NRG robes are instead decorated pink.

LIKE FATHER, UNLIKE SON
Cole and his dad share a rocky past. Cole's dad hoped that Cole would grow up to share his profession—dancing. Unwilling to upset him and wanting to become a ninja, Cole ran away. However, after rescuing his dad from Pythor, their relationship is restored and Cole unlocks his NRG status.

LEADER COLE is the third ninja to find his full potential. To progress on from Kendo level, Cole must mend his relationship with his father. By way of celebration for achieving this and becoming a NRG ninja, Cole's NRG outfit is much brighter than all of his previous variants—it is black and pink!

NRG KAI
TOO HOT TO HANDLE

Having mastered his element, Kai's eyes glow red with fire energy, not anger or jealousy.

NINJA FILE

LIKES: Being the best
DISLIKES: Helping Lloyd
FRIENDS: NRG ninja
FOES: His own jealousy
SKILLS: Complete mastery of fire
GEAR: Elemental power

SET NAME: Weapon Pack
SET NUMBER: 9591
YEAR: 2012

A red-hot fireball fittingly decorates Kai's NRG robes.

Sparks and flames descend on Kai's legs.

SPIN IT TO WIN IT
Kai tests his full potential in a Spinjitzu battle with the snake Chokun. The Serpentine can also use Spinjitzu skills in battle, but Chokun's powers do not match the well-trained Kai.

TO PROGRESS to the highest level along with his fellow ninja, Kai must learn to control his fiery temper. This is difficult for the hot-headed Master of Fire! When he learns to be himself, without being jealous of Lloyd's Green Ninja powers, Kai is the last, but by no means least, to reach full potential.

SEASON TWO of NINJAGO™: Masters of Spinjitzu sees the ninja, joined by Green Ninja Lloyd, thwart Lord Garmadon—only for him to rise again! But evil Garmadon has not returned alone. A devious entity called the Overlord and his dangerous Stone Army have arrived. A total of seven exciting sets bring the adventure alive with new bikes, blades, and baddies!

MY BLADE WILL SHATTER YOUR ARMY!

KIMONO KAI

ELEMENTAL FIRE NINJA

NINJA FILE

LIKES: His Fire Mech
DISLIKES: Fighting evil Nya
FRIENDS: Kimono ninja
FOES: Greedy Overlords
SKILLS: Fighting off
Garmadon's scouts
GEAR: Elemental
Fire Blade

SET NAME: Kai's Fire Mech
SET NUMBER: 70500
YEAR: 2013

Warrior head
wrap with gold
three-point
crown visor

DID YOU KNOW?
This version of Kai,
wearing his elemental
robes, is quite rare, as it
can only be found in
Kai's Fire Mech
(set 70500).

MAJOR FIREPOWER!
The awesome Fire Mech's huge
robot form has impenetrable
armor, cannons, katana swords,
and serrated blades. Kai pilots
it from a cockpit at the top.

Double-edged
elemental
Blade of Fire

Elemental
kimono with
sash complete
with fire symbo
on the back

IN THE TEMPLE OF LIGHT, fiery Kai gets
his elemental powers back and his new
kimono-style robe reflects the powerful
energy now coursing through him. Red-hot
Kai is ready to fight the Overlord's Stone
Warriors in his mighty Fire Mech, in a titanic
battle for control of the four elemental blades.

KIMONO JAY
ELEMENTAL LIGHTNING NINJA

Elemental kimono
with sash and
lightning symbol
on the back

Elemental
Lightning Blade

TEMPLE OF LIGHT TRANSFORMATION
When Lloyd strikes the bell in the Temple of Light, the energy produced raises the ninja to a higher elemental status. Jay regains his power over lightning and his sword manifests a blade representing this element.

DID YOU KNOW?
Jay uses a jet pack to escape from the Stone Warrior, who is in hot pursuit on his Warrior Bike (set 70501).

JAY LEADS THE NINJA to the Temple of Light, where he undergoes his transformation and wears a striking new elemental kimono to reflect his elevated status. He is once again master of his element and will need his fast reflexes to protect the elemental Lightning Blade.

KIMONO COLE

ELEMENTAL EARTH NINJA

NINJA FILE

LIKES: Defeating the Stone Warriors
DISLIKES: Losing his elemental Earth Blade
FRIENDS: Kimono ninja
FOES: Stone Swordsman
SKILLS: Deadly drilling
GEAR: Elemental Earth Blade

SET NAME: Cole's Earth Driller
SET NUMBER: 70502
YEAR: 2013

Ninja head wrap protects Cole's identity

Kimono in shades of Cole's trademark black colour

COLE'S EARTH DRILLER
This super-tough armored vehicle has a powerful rotating drill piece and can plough its way through any obstacle—including stone! With Cole in the driving seat, the ninja use these wheels to escape from the Stone Army.

Spinning drill piece

AFTER HAVING LOST but then regained his powers, Cole can't wait to take charge and see off the Stone Warriors. His sleek new kimono-style outfit is perfect for the job. Wielding the Earth Blade and harnessing his element, Cole is a force to be reckoned with. He has never been stronger.

KIMONO ZANE
ELEMENTAL ICE NINJA

Elemental kimono with sash and ice symbol on the back

Elemental Ice Blade

DID YOU KNOW?
Zane's elemental blade can generate frost and ice. It can fire freezing bolts and freeze things in place.

FALCON FRIEND
Zane's robot falcon was created by Zane's father, Dr. Julien, and first appears in LEGO form in set 70724. It shares a special bond with Zane and can communicate with him in his dreams. The Stone Army captures it, but Zane soon stealthily swoops to the rescue!

ZANE'S NEWLY ENHANCED POWERS
are as cool and icy as his new kimono-style ninja outfit. Armed with the double-edged Ice Blade, Zane is ready to freeze out the enemy—and he is able to produce an icy tornado powerful enough to knock even the Stone Warriors out cold!

LORD GARMADON
DARK ISLAND MASTER

NINJA FILE

LIKES: Giving orders
DISLIKES: Light
FRIENDS: General Kozu
FOES: The Green Ninja
SKILLS: Managing the
unruly Stone Army
GEAR: Mega-Weapon

SET NAME: Temple
of Light
SET NUMBER: 70505
YEAR: 2013

Helmet of
Shadows show
the Stone
Army's scorpi
claw symbol.

Removable
second torso with
two extra arms

ISLAND OF DARKNESS
When Lord Garmadon reads
about the Island of Darkness
in Captain Soto's log, he is
determined to find this evil place.

THE FORMIDABLE Master of Darkness has
not given up on his evil scheme to take over
Ninjago Island. Under the guidance of the
sinister Overlord, and looking more evil than
ever, Lord Garmadon has revenge on his
mind. He takes control of the Stone Army
on the Island of Darkness, ready to attack.

OVERLORD

GOLDEN MASTER

Full helmet with cheek guards

Spiked shoulder armor

Serrated blade weapon with red ax head

The Overlord is the only LEGO NINJAGO minifigure to wear a skirt piece.

THE DARK FALL OF NINJAGO ISLAND

In a combined attack, Lord Garmadon fires Dark Matter over the land, disrupting the balance between good and evil. It also allows the Overlord to escape while darkness infects the citizens.

FOR MANY YEARS nobody knew what the Overlord looked like in physical minifigure form. He had been spotted only as a dark shadow—trying to defeat goodness and bring evil to the world. Here he appears in his Golden Master form, proving this Overlord is a sinister shapeshifter!

GENERAL KOZU

STONE-FACED LEADER

NINJA FILE

LIKES: Bullying his troops
DISLIKES: Being chased by Zane's Ice Spider
FRIENDS: Lord Garmadon
FOES: Zane and the ninja
SKILLS: Multitasking at least four things at once
GEAR: Butterfly swords

SET NAME: Garmatron
SET NUMBER: 70504
YEAR: 2013

Samurai-style helmet features Stone Army decoration

Unique torso extension piece gives Kozu his extra arms

DID YOU KNOW?

The Stone Army soldiers speak a mysterious language of their own. General Kozu acts as their translator.

THE ULTIMATE WEAPON

The Garmatron—a caterpillar-tracked battle machine—can push aside anything in its path. Armed with a front cannon and side turrets to fire missiles, Kozu feels on top of the world from the driving seat.

Stone-grey detailing covers Kozu's belt, legs, and torso.

GENERAL KOZU is Lord Garmadon's second-in-command in the Stone Army. An experienced warrior, he is especially fearsome when his four arms are wielding four weapons all at once. Kozu is in charge of mining for Dark Matter and likes to keep busy—he uses his extra limbs to bully his troops.

STONE ARMY WARRIOR

UNDERWORLD SOLDIER ON THE UP

NINJA FILE

LIKES: Following orders
DISLIKES: Obstacles in his path to destruction
FRIENDS: Stone Warriors
FOES: Anyone "good"
SKILLS: Swordplay
GEAR: Butterfly sword, katana

SET NAME: Warrior Bike, The Golden Dragon
SET NUMBER: 70501, 70503
YEAR: 2013

As befits his rank, the warrior wears a winged helmet similar to Kozu's.

Ridged shoulder armor is common for Stone Army warriors and swordsmen.

FORCES OF DARKNESS
Originally created to defeat the First Spinjitzu Master and destroy all goodness in the land, the Stone Army is back in full force. The troops begin their mission massed on the Island of Darkness, waiting for their orders to roll out and take over Ninjago Island.

The warrior wields his butterfly sword in one hand and his katana in the other.

WHEN THE STONE ARMY was created by the Overlord, this tough warrior was built out of indestructible stone from the Underworld. Like his fellow soldiers, he is a tough-as-rock battle machine. He is rigidly unbending in his obedience, always follows orders and would love to crush the ninja.

STONE SWORDSMEN

WEAPON-WIELDING FIGHTER

Open mouth reveals sharp teeth and a grimace

Green swirl pattern marks all of the troops in the Stone Army

Silver chainmail on torso and kneepads on legs worn for protection

NINJA FILE

LIKES: Leading an assault
DISLIKES: Cole's drill
FRIENDS: Swordsmen
FOES: Cole and the ninja
SKILLS: Extreme swordsplay
GEAR: Black katana

SET NAME: Cole's Earth Driller, Garmatron, Temple of Light
SET NUMBER: 70502, 70504, 70505
YEAR: 2013

ALL YELLOW
This swordsman may look similar, but under the brim of his hat are yellow, not blue, markings. Rarer than his blue-faced counterparts, but just as ferocious, he can be found in one exclusive set: Samurai Accessory Set (850632).

THE STONE ARMY'S elite swordsmen are brutal, bulldozing fighters. Armed with their curved-edged, sharp-pointed katana swords, the Stone Swordsmen can deliver devastating cutting strokes to their enemies! The ninja will need all their sword skills and some strong armor in order to fight back.

Yellow and blue facial markings follow different patterns

STONE ARMY SCOUT

BOULDER-LIKE BOWMAN

DID YOU KNOW?

Both the scouts and the swordsmen wear conical hats like Master Wu's, but painted red exclusively for the Stone Army.

NINJA FILE

LIKES: Stealing weapons
DISLIKES: Getting lost
FRIENDS: Scouts
FOES: The ninja and the Golden Dragon
SKILLS: Perfect aim
GEAR: Crossbow

SET NAME: Kai's Fire Mech, The Golden Dragon, Temple of Light
SET NUMBER: 70500, 70503, 70505
YEAR: 2013

Arrow quiver worn across shoulder

Scouts have shorter legs than the swordsmen.

Standard LEGO crossbow

BLUE IN THE FACE

The blue-faced scout is so good at his job that you might find it difficult to spot him! Alongside the yellow-faced Swordsman, he only appears in set 850632.

ALTHOUGH SHORT-LEGGED, with their crossbows at the ready, the Stone Army scouts are a fearsome sight to behold. Before you can say "Bullseye!", this soldier will have loaded and shot several arrows. The scouts are a stealthy breed, as their primary role is to spy on enemy terrain.

91

TO STOMP WITH THE STONE ARMY YOU MUST:

SHOW FIERCE LOYALTY TO THE OVERLORD

POSSESS INDESTRUCTIBLE STRENGTH

HAVE A THICK SKULL AND STRONG FISTS

GIVE STONY LOOKS TO THE NINJA

GOLDEN NINJA
ULTIMATE SPINJITZU MASTER

NINJA FILE

LIKES: Defending Ninjago
DISLIKES: Catapults
FRIENDS: Golden Dragon
FOES: The Overlord
SKILLS: Summoning the Golden Dragon
GEAR: Golden Mech Sword

SET NAME: The Golden Dragon, Temple of Light
SET NUMBER: 70503, 70505
YEAR: 2013

Golden robes have the same pattern as one of his Green Ninja variants.

Even Lloyd's face and hands become gold when he harnesses the Golden Power!

DID YOU KNOW?
The Golden Power is a combination of all the main Elements of Ninjago: fire, earth, lightning, ice, and energy.

THE GOLDEN TOUCH
This ancient fighting Mech will only respond to the Golden Ninja's powers. Alongside the Golden Dragon, Lloyd finds it and awakens it in the Temple of Light.

Lloyd's seat in the cockpit is shaded by an oversized golden conical hat.

LLOYD GARMADON becomes the Golden Ninja after his first battle with the Overlord. He is now the most powerful ninja of all. His shimmering golden robe and armor are symbolic of his status and his potential to harness the Golden Power. With this upgrade he can overthrow the Overlord!

GOLDEN DRAGON
LEGENDARY SPINJITZU CREATURE

NINJA FILE

LIKES: Flying into battle
DISLIKES: Evil minions
FRIENDS: Master Lloyd
FOES: The Stone Army
SKILLS: Bellowing fire
GEAR: Dragon sphere

SET NAME: The Golden Dragon
SET NUMBER: 70503
YEAR: 2013

Lloyd rides the Golden Dragon from a white saddle flanked by flags.

Jaws can open wide to release sphere missile

DRAGON POWER!
Equipped with a cannon within its jaws, the magnificent Golden Dragon can fire dragon sphere missiles at the enemy! This dragon is a formidable battle machine, with huge extendable wings shaped like razor-sharp claws.

Head mold is the same as Cole's Earth Dragon, but painted gold with distinct green markings.

Long golden blade pieces uniquely used for fannable wings

AS THE GOLDEN NINJA, Lloyd uses his Golden Power to summon the mighty and mysterious Golden Dragon to battle by his side. He harnesses the creature's powers at the Temple of Light, and together, with their powers combined, they drive away the Stone Army and defeat the Overlord.

NINJA VS. THE OVERLORD AND HIS NINDROIDS

IN SEASON THREE of NINJAGO™: Masters of Spinjitzu the exciting New Ninjago City becomes the battleground for an epic clash between ninja and the Overlord. An army of the Overlord's Nindroids is advancing and it will take an unforgettable sacrifice to save Ninjago Island. Join the ninja in their fight against the Nindroids in a total of ten high-tech sets featuring scary villains and new, powerful weapons!

A TRUE NINJA NEVER GIVES UP!

MASTER GHRMADON

SPINJITZU MASTER REBORN

Simple bo staff used for berating students, not fighting.

Garmadon's evil activities have turned his hair gray.

NINJA FILE

LIKES: Being good again
DISLIKES: His evil past
FRIENDS: Brother Wu
FOES: Digital Overlord
SKILLS: Teaching ninja
GEAR: Bo staff

SET NAME: Nindroid Mech Dragon
SET NUMBER: 70725
YEAR: 2014

Flowing robes decorated with a golden clasp and ancient writings

NINJA MENTOR
Dressed in variant robes from Ninja DBX (set 70750), Master Garmadon enjoys teaching the Art of the Silent Fist—a martial arts style involving misdirection and avoiding enemy attacks.

A tear in the back of the robes reveals a purple snake tattoo.

COMPLETELY PURIFIED of evil, Garmadon transforms back into a man when the Overlord is seemingly defeated by Lloyd, the Golden Ninja. His extra arms and dark-lord armor disappear, along with the dark magic that possessed him, to be replaced by the ninja robes of a peace-loving Spinjitzu Master.

THE OVERBORG

POSSESSED COMPUTER GENIUS

NINJA FILE

LIKES: Inventing gadgets
DISLIKES: Being controlled like a machine
FRIENDS: Techno Zane
FOES: The Overlord
SKILLS: Chasing
GEAR: Katana, saw

SET NAME: OverBorg Attack
SET NUMBER: 70722
YEAR: 2014

Dual-sided head shows Cyrus Borg has not gone for good.

Hairpiece with robotic parts and cybernetic eyepiece

Saw-bladed weapon is common amongst the Nindroids.

A spider-legged mech transports the OverBorg around Ninjago.

TOWN PLANNER
After the first defeat of the Overlord, Cyrus Borg strove to make Ninjago Island a center of technological advancement. He rebuilt Ninjago City and named it "New Ninjago City."

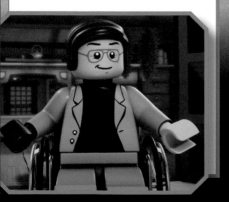

CYRUS BORG is an inventor, computer genius, and upstanding Ninjago citizen. But a bite from Pythor turns him into a cyber robot, controlled by the now-digital Overlord. Transformed into OverBorg, he uses his technological skills to summon the Nindroid Army in an attempt to rule Ninjago Island.

T: CHNO COL:
REBOOTED EARTH NINJA

NINJA FILE

LIKES: New technology
DISLIKES: Hover Hunters
FRIENDS: Techno ninja
FOES: General Cryptor
SKILLS: Converting Security
Mechs into Earth Mechs
GEAR: Green Techno-Blade

SET NAME: Hover Hunter,
Thunder Raider
SET NUMBER: 70720,
70723
YEAR: 2014

This is one of only two Cole minifigures to show his hair.

Cole's Techno-Blade resembles a set of nunchuks.

DID YOU KNOW?
The Techno-Blades can hack into computer systems and transform ordinary machinery into awesome hi-tech ninja vehicles.

COLE'S EARTH MECH
Cole pilots his Earth Mech from a small cockpit at the top of the huge robot, and fires missiles at his foes from the sword blasters on its arms.

DRESSED IN HIS STYLISH black Techno robes, with a matching bandana to help block facial-recognition software, Cole is ready to battle this latest enemy, the Nindroids. He loves a challenge and will push his ninja skills to their limits using the new techno gear—including his chained Techno-Blade.

High-powered sword blaster

TECHNO KAI
REBOOTED FIRE NINJA

NINJA FILE

LIKES: Transforming cars into weapons
DISLIKES: Insects
FRIENDS: Techno ninja
FOES: General Cryptor
SKILLS: Aiming missiles
GEAR: Red Techno-Blade

SET NAME: Kai Fighter, Ninja Charger
SET NUMBER: 70721, 70727
YEAR: 2014

Bandana disrupts facial-recognition software

Scarlet Techno-Blade

Techno robes with printed flame design

DID YOU KNOW?
Kai's X-1 Ninja Charger vehicle also has a built-in Recon Nindroid with jagged blades for aerial battle.

ON THE CHARGE
Watch out Nindroids! In his awesome X-1 Ninja Charger, Kai is a formidable opponent. This super car is decked out with missiles and a dual shooter in the central engine bay. Lift the hood to activate the built-in interceptor bike.

KAI'S FLAMING TECHNO SUIT
complements his fiery fighting style. He wears a matching red bandana to hide his face, but his hair is uncovered, like all of the Techno ninja. With his new sword-like Techno-Blade, Kai will channel all his strength to fight the sinister Nindroid Army.

TECHNO JAY
REBOOTED LIGHTNING NINJA

Each Techno-Blade is a different color—Jay's is lightning yellow.

NINJA FILE

LIKES: His off-roader
DISLIKES: The Nindroid's double laser cannon
FRIENDS: Techno ninja
FOES: Nindroids
SKILLS: Maneuvering the Thunder Raider
GEAR: Yellow Techno-Blade

SET NAME: Thunder Raider
SET NUMBER: 70723
YEAR: 2014

DID YOU KNOW?

Jay falls out with Cole when he discovers that Nya has feelings for the Earth Ninja as well as him.

New robe design, featuring streaks of lightning

THUNDER AND LIGHTNING

Jay's super-fast off-roader is a highly versatile ninja vehicle. The high-grip front tank treads and huge rear wheels power effortlessly over rough terrain at high speed.

In attack mode, the Thunder Raider fires hidden missiles.

JAY CAN MOVE at lightning speed, so his new Techno robes are extra mobile and decorated with electric-blue streaks of lightning. Just as quick with his brain, creative Jay always knows how to use his chainsaw Techno-Blade to its full effect. Go, ninja!

T: CHNO ZAN:
ROBOTIC NINJA OF ICE

NINJA FILE

LIKES: Flying his glider
DISLIKES: Nindroids
FRIENDS: P.I.X.A.L.
FOES: Nindroid army
SKILLS: Piloting
GEAR: Techno-Blade and shield, katana blades

SET NAME: Battle for Ninjago City
SET NUMBER: 70728
YEAR: 2014

To fight the Nindroids, Zane wields a blue Techno-Blade.

BATTLE-SCARRED
During battle with the Nindroids, in NinjaCopter (set 70724), Zane is badly damaged—seemingly beyond repair. But in Destructoid (set 70726), he appears rebooted, with his robotic parts hidden again!

LEARNING ABOUT HIS PAST only helps to make Zane a better ninja. Having reached his full potential, he is quick to locate his Techno-Blade—and even quicker to use it against the invading Nindroids. However, will he be strong enough to return after he is injured in battle?

TECHNO LLOYD

REBOOTED GREEN NINJA

Golden shoulder armor with scabbard for two katanas

DID YOU KNOW?

Lloyd's Techno suit is a mixture of all four of his previous ninja suits, with green legs and gold armor.

Techno suit with Golden Power emblem front and back

NINJA FILE

LIKES: Riding his Ninja Cycle
DISLIKES: Retreating
FRIENDS: His father—Master Garmadon
FOES: The OverBorg
SKILLS: Crushing Nindroids with his bike
GEAR: Golden swords

SET NAME: OverBorg Attack
SET NUMBER: 70722
YEAR: 2014

GREEN NINJA CYCLE

Zooming around on his Ninja Cycle, Techno Lloyd becomes a green and gold blur. The Overborg won't be able to catch him on this super slick machine.

Green and gold color scheme to match Lloyd's robes

THE GREEN NINJA is more powerful than ever and master of his Golden Power. His new Techno suit is emblazoned front and back with the Golden Power emblem, proudly showing off his elevated ninja status. With his golden armor and weapons, Techno Lloyd is primed for battle with the Overlord.

SAMURAI X
PHOENIX FLAME WARRIOR

Samurai helmet with ornamental spiked crest

Silver katana helps in fighting evil Nindroids

All-new armor with phoenix emblem

DID YOU KNOW?

Nya's helmet and face mask were new molds, created for Nya's 2012 Samurai X armor.

SAMURAI VS. NINDROIDS

Disguised as the mysterious warrior Samurai X, Nya shows the Nindroids what an accomplished and fierce fighter she is with her stealthy samurai moves!

NOT MANY PEOPLE know of Nya's secret identity. This smart girl is not only a superb engineer, but a skilled sword fighter too! She becomes Samurai X so she can fight alongside the boys, and her elaborate samurai armor and crested helmet reflect her warrior status.

TECHNO WU
GOOD MASTER GONE BAD

Traditional conical hat now looks like it is made out of metal, not bamboo.

Evil, red robot eyes

Black and white robe displays cyber robot parts.

NINJA FILE

LIKES: Flying the MechDragon
DISLIKES: Ninja escaping in Nya's car
FRIENDS: Pythor
FOES: All his old friends
SKILLS: Battling Garmadon
GEAR: Black bo staff

SET NAME: Nindroid MechDragon
SET NUMBER: 70725
YEAR: 2014

VICTIM OF THE OVERLORD
The Overlord probes Master Wu's memory to find out where the ninja are hiding. He then turns Wu into his latest cyber drone victim—Techno Wu—and forces him to attack the ninja and Garmadon. This is a battle the ninja don't want to have to fight.

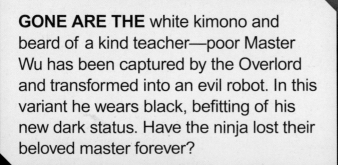

GONE ARE THE white kimono and beard of a kind teacher—poor Master Wu has been captured by the Overlord and transformed into an evil robot. In this variant he wears black, befitting of his new dark status. Have the ninja lost their beloved master forever?

P.I.X.A.L.
ACE ANDROID

The other side of P.I.X.A.L.'s face reveals a scowl and red eyes to show that she is under the Overlord's control.

NINJA FILE

LIKES: Puzzles
DISLIKES: Nindroids
FRIENDS: Zane
FOES: Digital Overlord
SKILLS: Using technology
GEAR: Spike blade

SET NAME: NinjaCopter
SET NUMBER: 70724
YEAR: 2014

Spike blade is similar to the saw blades commonly used by Nindroids.

FRIENDS FOR LIFE
P.I.X.A.L. changes from cold and mechanical to loyal friend when Zane uses his Techno-Blade to hack her programming. They go on to destroy many Nindroids together. When Zane is hurt, the two discover they are compatible and merge into one being—a move that saves Zane's life!

AS AN ANDROID, P.I.X.A.L. (Primary Interactive X-ternal Assistant Life-form) is a robot. While under the control of the Digital Overlord, she copies Zane's mechanisms to make the Nindroid Army. But she is eventually freed from her programming and changes her ways.

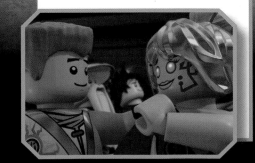

HOW TO CREATE YOUR OWN NINDROID ARMY:

BECOME AN EXPERT HACKER

MASTER THE DIGIVERSE

CHOOSE LOGIC OVER EMOTION

BE SMART IN YOUR ATTACKS

GENERAL CRYPTOR
LEADER OF THE NINDROID ARMY

Ninja wrap with attached robot eye piece

Ground-to-air laser rocket launcher

Sinister red buttons for firing lasers

DESTRUCTIVE DESTRUCTOID
General Cryptor controls his battle tank from its 360-degree rotating command center. He unleashes lasers and missiles from the disc shooter and uses the razor-sharp chopping blades to attack the enemy.

SECOND-IN-COMMAND to the Overlord, the talkative and quick-tempered General Cryptor is the most powerful and advanced of the Nindroids, reflected by his unique armor. Cryptor believes himself to be the greatest warrior in the world and tends to severely underestimate his enemies!

NINDROID WARRIOR

HIGH-TECH FIGHTING MACHINE

Kimono robe with exposed cyber robot parts

Double laser blades

AERIAL ATTACK

The Nindroid warrior from Nindroid MechDragon, (set 70725) launches an air attack on the ninja wearing a jet pack and wielding an axe-chainsaw spear.

THE NINDROID WARRIOR is a mechanical soldier modeled on Zane's programming. This result is a stronger, faster and more agile fighter than Zane, but lacking in emotions. Its only mission is to fight the ninja and follow orders from its master, the Overlord.

NINDROID DRONE

MINDLESS ROBOTIC TROOPER

The drone has the same head piece as the warrior—with a vertically split mechanical face.

A silver sai—the drone's weapon of choice

GLIDING INTO BATTLE

In a thrilling aerial battle in set 70724, the Nindroid Army attacks with their Jet Fighter. It deploys its detachable attack glider, which carries an ax-wielding Nindroid drone with a special neck brace.

DID YOU KNOW?

The Nindroid warrior and the drone show different robot parts on their torsos. Both have the saw blade emblem on their backs.

THE FEROCIOUS-LOOKING, red-eyed drone is a formidable robot soldier in the Nindroid Army. Unlike the Nindroid warrior, the drone doesn't wear a helmet, so its cyber head is fully exposed. This Nindroid is an accomplished fighter with the three-pronged sai.

MINDROID
SMALL SIZE, BIG TROUBLE!

The Mindroid wears a Nindroid warrior mask but has a drone torso.

NINJA FILE

LIKES: Getting angry
DISLIKES: Being teased for his height
FRIENDS: Techno Wu
FOES: Big bullies and ninja
SKILLS: Ninja Destruction!
GEAR: Techno Dagger

SET NAME: Destructoid
SET NUMBER: 70726
YEAR: 2014

Techno-Dagger sword

Mindroid is the only Nindroid with short legs

AROUND AND AROUND
The Nindroid Army has an arsenal of attack vehicles—such as the Hover Hunter and the Disc Flyer. All feature a rotating saw blade— a terrifying circular, serrated weapon.

IN SPITE OF HIS reduced size, the Mindroid has excellent combat skills. General Cryptor gave him his nickname, but the Mindroid is sensitive about his appearance and is quick to get angry when insulted. He doesn't have a voice, so instead communicates by making electronic beeps.

DARETH
THE "BROWN NINJA"

NINJA FILE

LIKES: Attention
DISLIKES: Being clumsy
FRIENDS: Adventurous ninja
FOES: Only villains
SKILLS: Stealing blades
GEAR: Shovel, trophy...
anything goes!

SET NAME: Dareth vs.
Nindroid (polybag)
SET NUMBER: 5002144
YEAR: 2014

Dareth admits that all his kung fu trophies are fake.

STREET URBAN MOJO DOJO!
Dareth owns a small dojo in New Ninjago City called the "Mojo Dojo". Dareth befriends the ninja when they ask him if they can use his dojo to train Lloyd.

Ninja robe over an open-necked shirt, with fleur-de-lis patterns on the legs

SPORTING SLICKED-BACK glossy hair and a gold medallion, the laid-back Dareth is a self-proclaimed kung fu master. However, it is soon blatantly obvious to the ninja that Dareth has no fighting skills whatsoever! They tease their new friend and dub him the "Brown Ninja" because of the color of his robes.

MASTER WU

REBOOTED

Golden bamboo conical hat

DID YOU KNOW?

The flower emblem on Wu's various ninja robes is the Ninjago symbol for destiny.

Wu's traditional bo staff

Exclusive Wu minifigure in new decorative robe

GOLD-EDGED GI

Master Wu's new exclusive robe is trimmed with ornate gold borders, flower emblems, and a gold sash belt. The back of the gi features a large gold flower emblem.

HE'S BACK! With the Overlord gone for the time being, Master Wu is restored to his normal wise and good self. But there is no time to rest—employing all of his skills, Wu must lead his ninja into another dangerous battle to destroy the Golden Master (the Digital Overlord) forever.

NINJA VS. MASTER CHEN AND HIS ANACONDRAI ARMY

SEASON FOUR of NINJAGO™: Masters of Spinjitzu sees the ninja scatter after the loss of their friend Zane. It takes an invitation to the Tournament of Elements to bring them back together. Join the ninja on their journey to a mysterious island. New dangers, new friends, and a big surprise await the ninja in a total of 14 sets.

NOT UNTIL I TEACH YOU A FINAL LESSON!

MASTER CHEN
LEADER OF THE ANACONDRAI

Anacondrai skull and spine piece on head, with large purple snake around the skull

Distinctive face with mustache, goatee, and sideburns

Tooth necklace

NINJA FILE

LIKES: Wicked plans and complicated strategies
DISLIKES: Followers who are less intelligent
FRIENDS: Loyal Clouse
FOES: Non-Anacondrai
SKILLS: Tricking people
GEAR: Staff of Elements

SET NAME: Condrai Copter Attack, Enter the Serpent
SET NUMBER: 70746, 70749
YEAR: 2015

Robe with gold trim and snake scale patterns

STAFF OF ELEMENTS
Chen's staff has the Power of Absorption—it takes the user's elemental power and stores it in the crystal orb. The elements can then be used by whoever holds it.

HOT-TEMPERED CHEN is a master of deception. He organizes the Tournament of Elements after Zane dies, as a guise to steal the powers of the Elemental Masters. With their powers he plans to perform a spell that will turn his followers into Anacondrai—and then he will destroy Ninjago Island!

PYTHOR
ANACONDRAI SURVIVOR REBORN

Long, curved neck, unique amongst Serpentine

Jagged, dark blade is more stylish and heavier than a regular dagger.

NINJA FILE

LIKES: Peace and quiet
DISLIKES: Challenges to Serpentine race
FRIENDS: Noble ninja
FOES: New Anacondrai
SKILLS: Invisibility
GEAR: Bronze blade

SET NAME: Ninja DB X
SET NUMBER: 70750
YEAR: 2015

Head, body, and tail printing is now purple on a white background.

VILLAINS UNITE
Pythor is an excellent planner, and his sneaky and manipulative ways are just what Chen and the Overlord are looking for to help take over Ninjago Island. But first they must get past Master Garmadon!

THIS SNAKE LOOKS FAMILIAR!
After being inside the belly of the Great Devourer, Pythor has returned but has been bleached white. He wants to restore Serpentine dominance on Ninjago Island, so he allies with the Overlord to get revenge on the ninja.

TOURNAMENT KAI

FIERCE AND FIERY COMPETITOR

NINJA FILE

LIKES: Winning
DISLIKES: Secrets
FRIENDS: Skylor
FOES: Karlof, Chen
SKILLS: Building trust
GEAR: Double-edged
sword, scythe Jade Blade

SET NAME: Kai Drifter,
Jungle Trap, Dojo Showdown
SET NUMBER: 30293,
70752, 70756
YEAR: 2015

Golden
scythe

Gold badge with
fire symbol

ROUND ONE
When Kai and Karlof go head to
head in the tournament arena,
both are desperate to win the
powerful Jade Blade weapon.
Karlof grabs the blade in his
metal fist, but Kai removes the
fist and eliminates the Master
of Metal from the competition.

DID YOU KNOW?
Kai is the only ninja
to wield two types of Jade
Blade; one resembles a
two-edged sword, the
other resembles
a scythe.

DRESSED IN THE SLEEVELESS ROBES
given to him by Chen, Kai is ready to enter
the Tournament of Elements. The robe is
light—ideal for ninja parkour battle moves—
but has a padded chest plate for protection.
Kai is quick to enter the competition—not
stopping to think about Chen's motives.

TOURNAMENT COLE

TRICKED, THEN TRAPPED

NINJA FILE

LIKES: Reuniting with friends
DISLIKES: Mysterious trapdoors leading to prison, meals involving noodles
FRIENDS: Zane
FOES: Chen's henchmen
SKILLS: Escaping jail
GEAR: Scythe Jade Blade

SET NAME: Lava Falls
SET NUMBER: 70753
YEAR: 2015

Matching black bandana to disguise face

Scythe Jade Blade

Ninja gi decorated with chest strap shows the elemental symbols of Kai, Cole, Jay, and Lloyd.

NOODLE PRISON

Despite Cole's competence, he loses in the tournament. Chen's henchmen kidnap him and put him in a cell in the underground dungeons. His elemental powers are taken from him and he is set to work in the Noodle Factory!

ARMED WITH A SCYTHE JADE BLADE, and all in black, Cole looks as serious as ever. With planned moves and strategic thinking, Cole combines his weapon skills and strength to show the competition what he is made of. However, he will need more than new robes to get out of Chen's trap!

TOURNAMENT JAY

UNLUCKY IN LOVE

NINJA FILE

LIKES: Defeating evil
DISLIKES: Fighting with his friends
FRIENDS: Nya
FOES: Cole, Chen
SKILLS: Extreme speed and agility
GEAR: Spear Jade Blade

SET NAME: Jay Nano Mech, ElectroMech
SET NUMBER: 30292, 70754
YEAR: 2015

Spear Jade Blade

DID YOU KNOW?
The green bladed end of the Jade Blade weapons represents the head of a dragon.

Printing on leg piece shows robe sash and knee stripes

LOVE FEUD
When Jay discovers that Cole has feelings for Nya too, he is angry with his friend. Chen takes advantage of this situation and pits the two ninja against each other in the tournament. From Chen's point of view, that takes two more ninja out of action.

JAY'S NEW LIGHT AND FLEXIBLE tournament robe is the perfect outfit to show off his ninja speed and agility in the competition arena. His opponents had better watch out—wielding his spear Jade Blade, Jay is a formidable combatant, both in and out of the tournament arena.

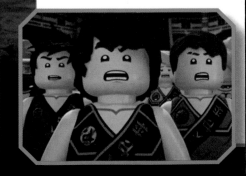

TOURNAMENT LLOYD

JUNGLE-BOUND

NINJA FILE

LIKES: Visiting new places, such as jungles and islands
DISLIKES: Causing mishaps
FRIENDS: Fearless Kai
FOES: Master Chen
SKILLS: Helping others
GEAR: Flail Jade Blade

SET NAME: Jungle Raider
SET NUMBER: 70755
YEAR: 2015

Flail Jade Blade is a nunchuk-style weapon.

JUNGLE RAIDER

Lloyd's cool, green off-roader, with its large, spiked wheels, is the perfect vehicle to travel through the rough terrain of the jungle. Armed with front shooters, the Green Ninja can battle the evil Anacondrai tribe.

LIKE HIS FELLOW NINJA, Lloyd's new tournament robes reflect his powerful combatant status. When he finds himself as the only remaining competitor, and has to fight Master Chen, he has to use all his elemental powers to defeat the evil leader.

CLOUSE

MASTER CHEN'S SECOND-IN-COMMAND

**DID YOU
KNOW?**
Clouse was one of the
masterminds behind
Chen's scheme to
transform himself and
his followers into
Anacondrai.

Shuriken and
snake fangs
pattern on
armor

Pike with four
side blades

CHEN'S STUDENT
Clouse studied alongside young
Garmadon under the training of
Master Chen. When a duel broke
out between the two students,
Chen declared that the winner
would become his right-hand
man. Garmadon cheated and
Clouse lost, for which Clouse
never forgave him.

THE SINISTER, PURPLE-ROBED CLOUSE
is a master of dark magic. He is a member of
Chen's Anacondrai Army and proudly wears
armor decorated with snake heads and fangs.
Once Chen has collected all the elements,
Clouse will use his evil dark magic to
transform the warriors into Anacondrai.

SKYLOR
ELEMENTAL MASTER OF AMBER

NINJA FILE

LIKES: The color red, mostly on Kai

DISLIKES: Devilish dads

FRIENDS: Kai

FOES: Anacondrai

SKILLS: Can absorb others' elemental powers

GEAR: Crossbow

SET NAME: Condrai Copter Attack

SET NUMBER: 70746

YEAR: 2015

Arrow and quiver

Japanese symbol represents the number 6—could Skylor become the sixth ninja?

DID YOU KNOW?

Skylor's mother was the previous Elemental Master of Amber, but no one knows what happened to her or where she has gone.

FAMILY TIES

During the tournament, it is revealed that Skylor is the daughter of Master Chen. When Skylor finds out how evil her father really is, she is torn between her daughterly loyalty towards him, and doing the right thing.

Knee pads on leg piece

SKYLOR'S ROBES reflect her elemental power—Amber, or energy assimilation. With a simple touch, Skylor can absorb other powers and make use of them herself. A trained ninja and highly skilled with the bow and arrow, Skylor enters the Tournament of Elements. But can she be trusted?

KARLOF

ELEMENTAL MASTER OF METAL

NINJA FILE

LIKES: Shiny metals
DISLIKES: The thought of losing a fight
FRIENDS: Opponent Cole
FOES: Thieving Skylor
SKILLS: Power-packed punching, engineering
GEAR: Metallic fists

SET NAME: Dojo Showdown
SET NUMBER: 70756
YEAR: 2015

Samurai helmet

Shoulder pad armour with scabbard for two katana swords

Metal fists also worn by Gorillas in LEGO® Legends of Chima™ sets.

Silver metal body armour worn over black robe

FIRST ONE OUT

Karlof loses to Kai in the first round of the tournament when Kai craftily steals the Jade Blade from him. He is taken to a secret underground room where Chen drains his metal power. Defenceless, Karlof is then set to work in Chen's Noodle Factory.

WHAT BRUTISH KARLOF lacks in ninja fighting skills, he makes up for with his strength and stamina. He can turn his body into hard metal and his hands into giant metal fists—all of which enhances his punching power! Karlof comes from Metalonia, where he worked as a mechanic and an engineer.

GRIFFIN TURNER

ELEMENTAL MASTER OF SPEED

Dual-sided head (angry face without shades on reverse)

Griffin wields a sturdy staff as his weapon.

Aerodynamic kimono

NINJA FILE

LIKES: Winning races
DISLIKES: Delays
FRIENDS: Ninja
FOES: That cheater Chen
SKILLS: Awesome speed, kick-boxing
GEAR: Bo staff

SET NAME: Dojo Showdown
SET NUMBER: 70756
YEAR: 2015

FASTER THAN FAST

Griffin likes to show off his elemental power and is extremely competitive. However, when he finds out what the evil Chen is really up to, he joins forces with the ninja.

DID YOU KNOW?

Griffin (along with Karlof and Skylor) is one of only three new Elemental Masters to appear in a LEGO set.

BLINK AND YOU'LL MISS HIM! Griffin Turner can run at incredible speeds. In his red sunglasses and his kimono adapted for running, Griffin thinks he is one cool dude. He makes it through several rounds of the tournament, until he is tricked by Chen and has his powers drained.

TO RAISE AN ANACONDRAI ARMY YOU MUST

PLAN AN EXCITING TOURNAMENT AS A DIVERSION

ATTRACT ELEMENTAL MASTERS TO A REMOTE LOCATION

STEAL POWERS FROM THE MASTERS TO COMPLETE AN ANCIENT SPE

WATCH YOUR ARMY TRANSFORM INTO MENACING SERPENTS

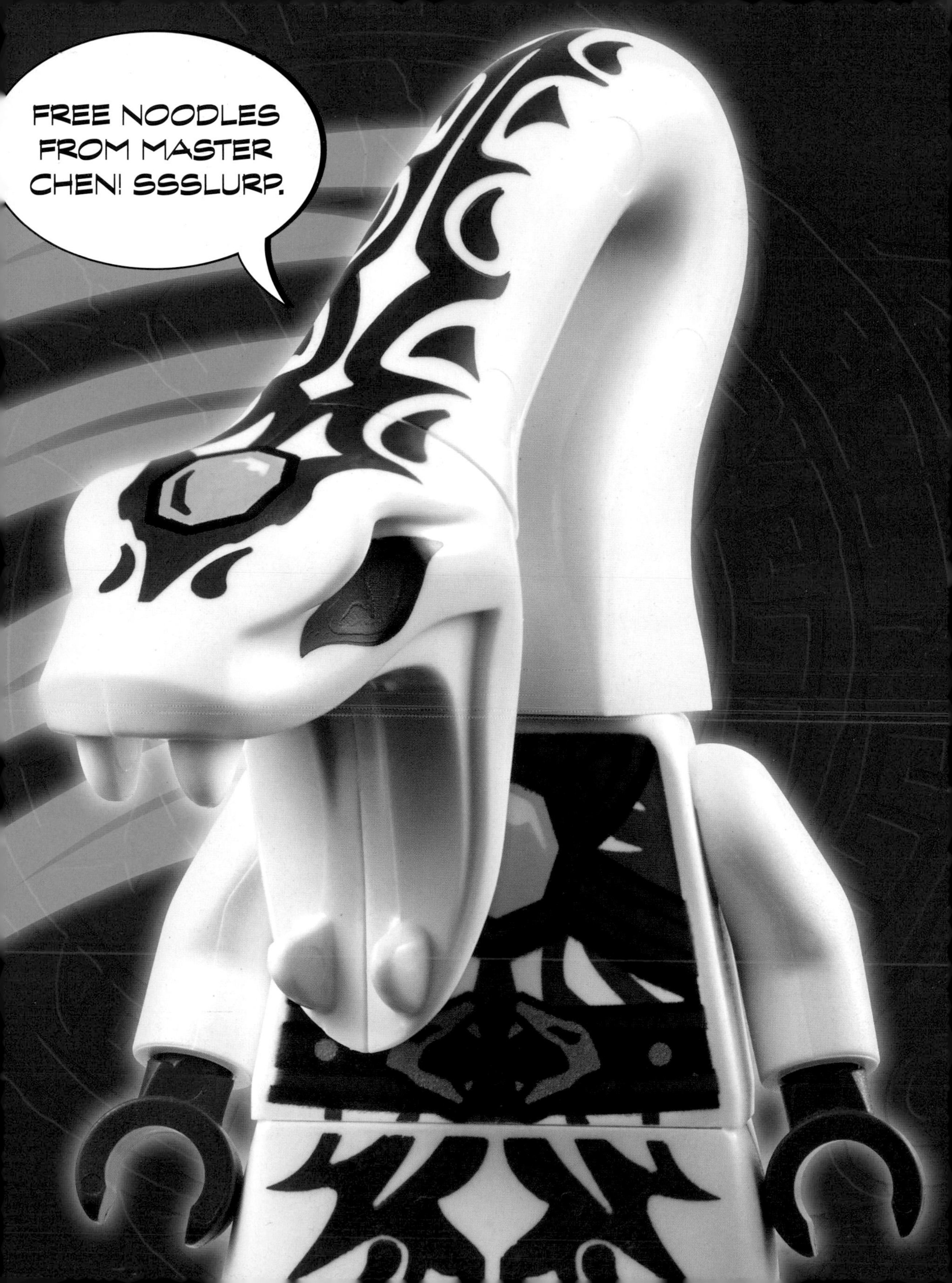
FREE NOODLES FROM MASTER CHEN! SSSLURP.

EYEZOR
CHIEF ANACONDRAI WARRIOR

Mohawk hair piece instead of the snake helmet worn by all other army members

Leather vest with snake-head belt buckle and snake tooth necklace

Eyezor's Anacondrai Blade is a bone sword with jagged purple edges.

Silver "punk" chains and buckles printed on legs

CONDRAI COPTER CHASE!
Eyezor pursues Skylor through the jungle in the fearsome-looking Condrai Copter, with its adjustable wings for flight or attack mode. Firing missiles, he swoops down to drop a net over his victim.

Huge net shoots out from snake's mouth

VICIOUS EYEZOR is Chen's lead thug and a general in his Anacondrai army. His "punkish" look makes his victims quiver. Eyezor is always happy to do Chen's dirty work. He helps to run the Noodle Factory—he guards the enslaved workers and makes sure they work hard and don't escape.

ZUGU
ANACONDRAI GENERAL

Anacondrai snake skull helmet

Anacondrai Blade is the main weapon used by the Anacondrai Army.

NINJA FILE

LIKES: Food
DISLIKES: Prison breaks
FRIENDS: Eyezor
FOES: All of the prisoners
SKILLS: Sumo-wrestling
GEAR: Anacondrai Blade

SET NAME: Boulder Blaster, Enter the Serpent
SET NUMBER: 70747, 70749
YEAR: 2015

DID YOU KNOW?

Even though the warriors resemble Anacondrai, they need the venom of a true Anacondrai (such as Pythor) to finish the spell.

NOODLE-ICIOUS!

Zugu oversees production of the goods in the Noodle Factory, which are then shipped to Chen's Noodle House in Ninjago City. He watches the prisoners closely to make sure they don't eat any of the mouth-watering noodles!

THE BRUTISH ZUGU used to be a Sumo wrestler, before rising through the ranks of Master Chen's secret Anacondrai army to become one of his two generals. His bulk and strength make him a formidable opponent. He and Eyezor take great pleasure in frightening their prisoners.

SLEVEN
ANACONDRAI PILOT

Snake tattoos on face and torso

Fang-shaped dagger

Snake-head belt buckle

NINJA FILE

LIKES: Master Chen
DISLIKES: Snakes... and turning into one
FRIENDS: Clouse, Chen
FOES: The speedy Griffin
SKILLS: Piloting mechs
GEAR: Scythe

SET NAME: Boulder Blaster, Lava Falls, Dojo Showdown
SET NUMBER: 70747, 70753, 70756
YEAR: 2015

FACE OFF
Sleven shares the same torso and leg pieces as his comrade-in-arms, Krait. The facial tattoos distinguish these two warriors, as do their expressions: Sleven shows bared teeth whereas Krait has a tight-lipped, scarred mouth.

DID YOU KNOW?
The Anacondrai have powers of invisibility. Skilled and ruthless warriors, this skill makes them unpredictable in combat!

SLEVEN IS A RATHER RELUCTANT warrior in Chen's Army—he's terrified of snakes and the thought of being turned into one makes him nervous. In spite of this phobia, Sleven is dedicated to Chen, and takes his job as pilot of the Anacondrai Battle Mech seriously.

CHOPE
ANACONDRAI WARRIOR

Full-face purple pattern tattoo

Snake tattoo and chest muscles on torso

NINJA FILE

LIKES: Flashy nicknames
DISLIKES: Receiving commands—he wants to be in charge, instead
FRIENDS: Buddy Kapau
FOES: All of the ninja
SKILLS: Climbing ranks
GEAR: Spear

SET NAME: ElectroMech
SET NUMBER: 70754
YEAR: 2015

DID YOU KNOW?
The original, and true, Anacondrai leaders had tails, but in their pre-transformed state, their new followers do not.

ELECTROMECH BATTLE
The evil Chope is no match for the skilful Master of Lightning, Jay, in his awesome ElectroMech with its huge grabbing fist and dual stud shooter. Hang on, Chope!

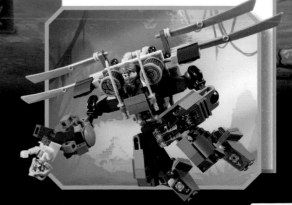

THUGGISH CHOPE IS HAPPY to follow his master's orders, however evil they are. He displays his Anacondrai serpent tattoo with pride. His loyalty to the Anacondrai mission has earned him a place in Chen's trusted inner circle of warriors, along with fellow soldier, Kapau.

KAPAU

AMBITIOUS ANACONDRAI

NINJA FILE

LIKES: Getting promoted
DISLIKES: Eyezor's jokes
FRIENDS: Chope
FOES: All of the ninja
SKILLS: Gaining power
GEAR: Double-headed fang dagger

SET NAME: Ninja DB X, Jungle Raider
SET NUMBER: 70750, 70755
YEAR: 2015

Bared fangs

SABOTAGE
Chen orders his minions to sabotage the Elemental Masters' hunt for the Jade Blades. Kapau and his best buddy, Chope, happily rise to the task, albeit leaving a trail of chaos behind them!

Double-headed fang-shaped blade dagger

WHAT HE LACKS in skills and talents, the vicious Kapau makes up for in ambition. When his dream of becoming one of Chen's chosen inner circle comes true, Kapau finds himself in way over his head. Not that this stops him trying to impress his master!

KRAIT

ANACONDRAI HENCHMAN

DID YOU KNOW?
All Anacondrai warrior minifigures have individual facial and body tattoos apart from Sleven and Krait, who share the same chest tattoos.

NINJA FILE

LIKES: Serpents
DISLIKES: Being fooled by the ninja in disguise
FRIENDS: Kapau, Eyezor
FOES: Elemental Masters
SKILLS: Chopping logs
GEAR: Skull ax

SET NAME: Anacondrai Crusher, Jungle Trap, Krait
SET NUMBER: 70745, 70752, 901503
YEAR: 2015

Scar running over lips

Krait's torso and leg pieces are the same as on the Sleven minifigure.

Double-bladed bone ax

S-S-S-SECRET DISGUISE

The ninja want to find out what Chen is up to. So after capturing four of Chen's warriors, they disguise themselves in their outfits, make Anacondrai tattoos out of chocolate, and sneak into the secret Anacondrai temple.

KRAIT IS ONE OF MASTER CHEN'S muscled henchmen, dedicated to Chen's every villainous whim, and completely committed to the cause of the Anacondrai Army. He is a ruthless fighter. The ninja will have to use their powers and skills to the full to battle this ax-wielding brute.

CHOP'RAI
CHOPE TRANSFORMED

NINJA FILE

LIKES: Slithering about
DISLIKES: Tough but slippery purple skin
FRIENDS: Kapu'rai
FOES: Master Wu—for organizing their defeat
SKILLS: Leading attacks
GEAR: Anacondrai Blade

SET NAME: Titanium Dragon, Ninja DB X
SET NUMBER: 70748, 70750
YEAR: 2015

Shoulder pad armor decorated with fang spikes

Bone sword with sharp, jagged edges on the blade

DID YOU KNOW?
The new Anacondrai are eventually banished to the Cursed Realm by some real Anacondrai ghosts, summoned by Master Wu.

TRANSFORMATION
Chope and Kapau complete the first part of the ritual of the ancient Anacondrai transformation spell from Clouse's spellbook in the Crystal Caves, where they are holding Skylor and Kai captive.

THE ANACONDRAI HAVE RETURNED!
Using Pythor's venom, the spell is completed and the warriors transform. Chope becomes the sly, blade-wielding serpent Chop'rai and his mission is to help Chen take over Ninjago. Will the Elemental Masters be able to defeat this new fearsome enemy?

KAPU'RAI
KAPAU TRANSFORMED

NINJA FILE

LIKES: His new tail
DISLIKES: Banishment to the Cursed Realm
FRIENDS: Chop'rai
FOES: All of Wu's army
SKILLS: Guarding prisons
GEAR: Anacondrai Blade

SET NAME: Enter the Serpent
SET NUMBER: 70749
YEAR: 2015

New head and tail pieces identical to Chop'rai's

DID YOU KNOW?
For the warriors' transformation to be permanent, they needed the venom of a true Anacondrai.

One red arm, just like his original form

Torso decorated with snake scales

SOLDIER TO SERPENT
In his transformed serpent state, Kapu'rai wears the same armor as in his original warrior form. However, when his legs are replaced by his huge new snake tail, his battle robes get torn and tattered.

WITH PYTHOR'S VENOM, Kapau is able to achieve his dream and becomes the terrifying armored snake, Kapu'rai. With fangs bared, and tail-pieces on trend again, Kapu'rai follows his master into the final showdown with the Elemental Masters in the Corridor of Elders.

JUNGLE KAI

GOING ON A SNAKE HUNT

NINJA FILE

LIKES: Playing hide and seek in the jungle

DISLIKES: Anyone who turns against their friends

FRIENDS: Skylor

FOES: Trickster Chen

SKILLS: Fooling Chen

GEAR: Golden swords

SET NAME: Anacondrai Crusher, Ninja DB X

SET NUMBER: 70745, 70750

YEAR: 2015

Bright red robes might not be best for hiding in the jungle!

Full-body gi with leather belt and chest pouch with fire emblem

Two kunai knives slot under leather scabbard chest strap

ELEMENTAL BOND

To Kai's overjoyed surprise, when he helps Skylor to escape from her father, she finally admits that she has feelings for him in return.

KAI AND HIS NINJA COMRADES must battle the loathsome Anacondrai in the thick jungle on Chen's deadly island. Luckily, Kai's new lightweight gi and zukin hood provide the perfect outfit for creeping stealthily through the undergrowth to ambush the Serpents.

JUNGLE COLE

ESCAPED PRISONER

Ninja zukin showing Cole's elemental symbol

DID YOU KNOW?
Chen's new Anacondrai Army hides out deep in the jungle. The ninja must follow the soldiers there to defeat them.

Arrowhead knife slots into leather scabbard chest strap

Leather kneepads

PRISON BREAKOUT
In his roto jet Boulder Blaster, Cole finally escapes from the Noodle Factory prison. He uses the eight-missile spring-loaded rapid shooter to blast through the walls and fly past the Anacondrai guards.

EVENTS ON CHEN'S ISLAND reveal Cole's inner strengths and his progression towards achieving true ninja awareness and spirit. Dressed in his new jungle battle attire, Cole is more determined than ever to rid Ninjago Island of this latest Serpent evil, whatever the cost to himself.

JUNGLE JAY
STUCK IN A TRAP

NINJA FILE

LIKES: Saving his friends
DISLIKES: Serpent traps
FRIENDS: Karlof
FOES: Sleven
SKILLS: Executing escape plans with swagger
GEAR: Golden sai

SET NAME: Enter the Serpent
SET NUMBER: 70749
YEAR: 2015

One of two golden sai

Full-body gi with leather belt and chest pouch with lightning emblem

DID YOU KNOW?
In the NINJAGO™ TV series, Jay is imprisoned in an underground part of the Anacondrai Temple.

DOWN AND OUT?
The Anacondrai are holding Jay captive in their temple deep in the jungle. Can the ninja dodge the spring-loaded shooters in the stairs, the poison balls, and the hidden trapdoors to rescue their friend?

THE JUNGLE IS TREACHEROUS, even for the speedy and inventive Master of Lightning. Jay's face is disguised by his jungle zukin and he is armed with two sai and two knives, but he will still need all of his creative and stealthy ninja skills to avoid the hidden Serpent traps.

JUNGLE LLOYD
MAP READER

Leather scabbard for two golden katana swords

NINJA FILE

LIKES: Unshakeable unity
DISLIKES: Heights!
FRIENDS: Green Dragon
FOES: Clouse
SKILLS: Coordinating attack teams
GEAR: Golden swords

SET NAME: Enter the Serpent
SET NUMBER: 70749
YEAR: 2015

Map with directions to Anacondrai temple

Flame torch

SPELLBOUND!
Lloyd will need all of his powers to battle giant Serpents, find his way to the jungle temple and stop Chen using the spell to transform his followers into Anacondrai. His map will show him the way...

GREEN NINJA LLOYD is kitted out in the perfect color for jungle adventures. It is his mission to stop more dark magic. Equipped with a flame torch, a map, weapons, and wearing his special jungle robes—which offer excellent camouflage amongst the trees—Lloyd can creep up on his slippery enemy!

NYA
MASTER OF DISGUISE

Samurai helmet with gold ornamental spiked crest

Face guard for protection and to hide identity

Nya's alternative samurai robe, and body armor is green with gold flames and a phoenix emblem.

KABUKI SPY
Resourceful Nya is a master of stealth and disguise. Dressed as a theatrical Kabuki girl, she sneaks into Chen's palace to find out what he is up to and to make contact with the ninja.

ON THE RUN FROM CHEN, his minions, and their Anacondrai transformation spell, Nya dons her fearsome-looking samurai armor and escapes into the jungle to find the ninja and warn them about Chen's evil plans. Leaving a fake trail of footprints, Nya eludes the enemy!

AUTO-PILOT ROBOT
DB X ROBOT DRIVER

Small blue head has golden binocular piece for eyes.

Gray pistol pieces used for arms

DID YOU KNOW?

The DBX's cloaking device alters the vehicle to look like either a noodle truck, a circus train, a school bus or a boulder.

Black skeleton pieces used for legs

ROBO UPGRADES
Nya is a talented mechanic. She built the D.B. Express (DBX), the ninja's mobile base complete with the auto-pilot robot and a cloaking device to alter the vehicle's appearance.

AUTO IS THE AUTO-PILOT ROBOT of the ninja's D.B. Express (DBX) vehicle. He can be activated to aid the driver in precarious situations. Taking control of the wheel in the front seat, he slides the driver into the back seat, freeing them up to fire missiles at the pursuing enemy.

TITANIUM ZANE

ICE NINJA REBUILT

NINJA FILE

LIKES: Embracing his new powers
DISLIKES: Fearing death
FRIENDS: Titanium Dragon
FOES: Clouse
SKILLS: Unleashing the Titanium Dragon
GEAR: Golden sai, katanas

SET NAME: Titanium Dragon
SET NUMBER: 70748
YEAR: 2015

Titanium shoulder pad armor with scabbard for two katana swords

Ninja zukin is a headwrap showing Zane's elemental symbol.

Two shurikens slot under titanium belt

TWICE TITANIUM

The new improved Titanium Zane has a dual-sided head with two Nindroid faces. One shows a happy, metallic robot face with blue eyes, whilst the other shows a serious Zane with a protective blue visor and robotic eyepiece.

UNKNOWN TO THE OTHER NINJA, when Zane was attacked by the Golden Master, he wasn't completely destroyed. A digital part remained, and Zane was able to rebuild himself as the Titanium Ninja. Dressed in cool titanium armor, Zane is shinier than ever, and ready to rejoin the ninja.

TIThNIUM DRAGUN

ZANE'S ELEMENTAL DRAGON

NINJA FILE

LIKES: Making Zane proud
DISLIKES: Losing a battle
FRIENDS: Titanium Zane
FOES: Anacondrai
SKILLS: Freezing the enemy
GEAR: Armored body

SET NAME:
Titanium Dragon
SET NUMBER:
70748
YEAR: 2015

Opening mouth with sharp teeth

Posable wings, legs, and tail

NIGHTMARE CREATURE!

The Titanium Dragon first appears to Zane in a nightmare. It is symbolic of his inner doubts and fear of death. Once he overcomes these fears, he is able to conjure the dragon at will and control it in reality.

THIS MONSTROUS DRAGON is a fearsome battle creature. Its huge body is covered in combat-scarred armored plates and spikes. It has sharp fangs and claws, and a spiked whip-like tail. Once Zane accepts that he is no longer just the Ice Ninja, he is able to control the beast.

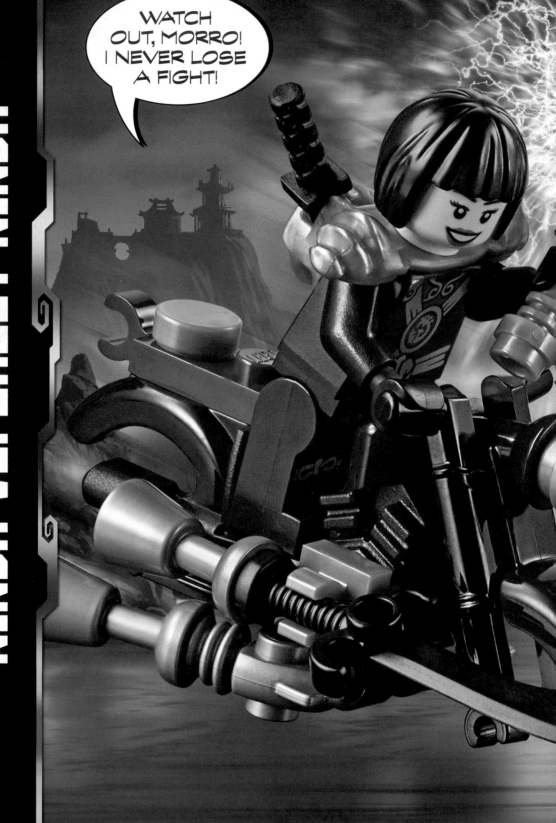

IN SEASON FIVE of NINJAGO™: Masters of Spinjitzu, a threat rises like none before. Ghosts swarm over Ninjago Island, possessing one ninja and turning another into a ghost! Old foes return and the ninja need all the help they can get to counter Morro, the Master of Wind. A total of 18 sets bring you thrilling minifigures and weapons that are bigger than any before!

I'LL PROVE YOU WRONG!

DEEPSTONE LLOYD

WAGING GHOST WARS

NINJA FILE

LIKES: Protecting Ninjago
DISLIKES: Being possessed
FRIENDS: Deepstone ninja
FOES: Morro
SKILLS: Patience
GEAR: Deepstone katana

SET NAME: Final Flight of Destiny's Bounty, Temple of Airjitzu
SET NUMBER: 70738, 70751
YEAR: 2015

New double-layered, two-colored zukin headwrap

Green Ninja's elemental symbol on front of torso, with h Creation emble on the back

Straps and belt in ninja's personal color

DEEPSTONE STYLE
Lloyd's Deepstone minifigure appears in two sets. He comes with his new zukin headwrap and his distinctive blond hairpiece for two interchangeable looks.

HAVING DEFEATED THE ANACONDRAI, Lloyd and his fellow ninja must now face the treacherous Morro and his Ghost Army. Lloyd is fired up to save Ninjago Island from these ghoulish creatures, but is his new Deepstone armor enough to protect him from the dark forces at work?

EVIL GREEN NINJA

POSSESSED!

Jagged-edged zukin headwrap with green bandana face mask attached

Sword of Sanctuary

FRIEND OR FOE?

The Evil Green Ninja attacks the ninja on the *Destiny's Bounty*, and tries to steal the Staff of the First Master of Spinjitzu. In a battle with Kai, the Master of Fire is able to momentarily remind Lloyd of his true self, before Morro takes control again.

DID YOU KNOW?

The Sword of Sanctuary has the power of precognition, which means the possessor of it can see into the future.

LLOYD BECOMES the evil Green Ninja when Morro possesses him. Manipulative Morro tricks Lloyd into a meeting at the Ninjago Museum of History and then takes control of his body. Lloyd takes on the ghoulish features of his possessor, and wears sinister, tattered robes.

DEEPSTONE JAY

GHOST HUNTER

NINJA FILE

LIKES: Eerie tombs
DISLIKES: Deadly tests
FRIENDS: Scaredy cat Cole
FOES: Bansha
SKILLS: Protecting friends
GEAR: Deepstone Nunchuk

SET NAME: Jay Walker One, City of Stiix, Attack of the Morro Dragon, Titan Mech Battle, Temple of Airjitzu
SET NUMBER: 70731, 70732, 70736, 70737, 70751
YEAR: 2015

DID YOU KNOW?

Deepstone, mined from the bottom of the ocean, is an effective material used in both combat and defense against the ghosts.

Two shurikens slot into belt

Deepstone Nunchuck

HAUNTED GATEWAY

Jay must get to the Haunted Gateway and grab the Aeroblade before Morro's ghost troops overpower him and turn him into a ghost, too!

WIELDING HIS DEEPSTONE Nunchuks at lightning speed, Jay is a formidable force. Kitted out in his sleek, protective robe and armor, Jay is calm and focused on his mission to get the Scroll of Airjitzu and to take on the testing challenges of the Haunted Temple.

DEEPSTONE KAI

AQUAPHOBIC

Zukin headwrap
in Kai's signature
red color

Deepstone
Scythe

TOMB RAIDERS

Kai jumps on his
speedy jet board to
try and intercept the
terrifying Morro
Dragon. Kai hopes to
stop the Evil Green
Ninja from stealing
the Realm Crystal
from the tomb of
the First Spinjitzu
Master.

Kai's elemental
symbol is on the
front of torso and
his fire emblem
on the back.

DID YOU KNOW?

The Aeroblades, circular
shuriken-like weapons,
have the ability to defeat
the ghosts when they
come into contact
with them.

FIERY KAI will do anything (even if it
means overcoming his fear of water!)
to save his friend Lloyd. Armed with
his Deepstone Scythe, Kai marches
to Stiix to take on the might of the
Ghost Army and destroy Morro and
his ghostly thugs.

DEEPSTONE ZANE

NINDROID VS. GHOSTS

Aeroblade—
when touched
it glows!

New black ninja robe with
body armor made from
Deepstone material protects
the wearer from being
possessed by the ghosts.

TITAN MECH BATTLE
Sitting in the cockpit of his Titan Mech,
Zane is set for the ultimate Mech
battle. He uses the awesome weapons
of his mighty machine to fight the
terrifying four-armed Ghost Mech,
Mech-enstein!

THE TITANIUM NINJA is back in style!
As cool as his icy element in his new
Deepstone gear, Zane uses his superior
robotic intelligence, stamina, and sixth
sense to the max to tackle and outwit the
ghostly enemy. With an Aeroblade at his
command, Zane is armed and dangerous!

DEEPSTONE COLE

GHOST VS. GHOSTS

New double-layered, two-coloured zukin headwrap

Deepstone Scythe

DEEPSTONE BLASTER BIKE
Cole's futuristic motorcycle was built by Cyrus Borg for Cole to use to fight the Ghost Warriors.

Barrel cannon on each side of bike to blast ghosts

A TRUE NINJA, Cole is calm and focused, using his combat skills and great strength to protect the ninja team against the terrifying Ghost Warriors. Overcoming his own fears, Cole always puts his friends' safety before his own.

MORRO

GHOST ELEMENTAL MASTER OF WIND

Bandana to hide identity

Ninja gi bearing the Golden Power emblem

Ragged black cape

Transparent green ghost legs

NINJA FILE

LIKES: Proving Wu wrong
DISLIKES: Taking selfies, losing the Realm Crystal
FRIENDS: Soul Archer
FOES: Lloyd
SKILLS: Airjitzu
GEAR: Howling Whip

SET NAME: Final Flight of Destiny's Bounty, Airjitzu Morro Flyer
SET NUMBER: 70738, 70743
YEAR: 2015

PERFECT STUDENT
Morro was Master Wu's first student. He soon mastered the martial arts and Wu thought that he might be the prophesied Green Ninja. When it became clear that he wasn't, Morro became obsessed with proving Wu wrong.

BACK FROM THE CURSED REALM as a ghost, Morro is set on revenge against Wu and the ninja. Driven by jealousy, Morro uses his cunning and mastery of his element, the wind, to possess Lloyd and attack the ninja. His mission is to bring evil to Ninjago Island once again.

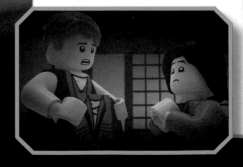

MORRO'S DRAGON

POSSESSED ELEMENTAL WIND DRAGON

Large articulated fabric wings

DID YOU KNOW?
Unlike the other ghost dragons, who only have ethereal snake-like bodies, Morro's possessed dragon has limbs and vicious claws, too.

Saddle has giant claw decorations with neon steering ghost chain.

Huge brick-built, posable head with opening fang-filled jaw

ARTICULATED MONSTER
Morro's dragon is a frightening sight with its neon fangs and claws. The beast's legs, feet, and whip-like tail have full articulation with ball hinges.

MORRO'S ONCE BENIGN

earthly elemental Wind Dragon is now a ferocious and vile ghost beast. The mighty creature is completely under Morro's dark control and will do whatever his evil master bids him to do, capturing his victims in his huge fang-filled jaws.

MASTER WU
IN RETIREMENT

Separate long beard and mustache

Flaming teapot

Deepstone Staff

DID YOU KNOW?
Master Wu's tea shop is called Steep Wisdom. It is located in a valley on Ninjago Island and has a tea farm and pond behind it.

TEA SHOP BREAK-IN
When the Ghost Warriors attack Wu's tea farm and shop, he comes out of retirement to help his ninja battle the attackers.

AFTER MASTER WU RETIRES, he opens a tea shop with the help of Nya and Misako. The wise old ninja enjoys drinking tea and sharing stories with his customers. However, his teaching days aren't entirely over— between cups of tea he trains Nya to become the Water Ninja.

MASTER WU'S DRAGON

ELEMENTAL CREATION DRAGON

Golden body armor made from conical hats

Detachable box saddle

Dragon features a large mustache and bushy eyebrows like its master.

NINJA FILE

LIKES: Being summoned
DISLIKES: Ghost poison
FRIENDS: Master Wu
FOES: Soul Archer
SKILLS: Firing missiles
GEAR: Fearsome jaws

SET NAME: Master Wu Dragon
SET NUMBER: 70734
YEAR: 2015

THIS MYSTICAL CREATURE is Master Wu's first Elemental Dragon. Even though he has had the skills to summon it for years, Wu calls on it for the first time to inspire Nya to become the Master of Water. He later calls on the beast to aid in the ninja's battles with the Ghost Warriors.

WOOF, WOOF!
Master Wu gets himself a pet dog when he retires. The dog helps him guard the tea shop and farm and Wu has even made him a special wheeled carriage to carry a crossbow!

RONIN
MERCENARY AND THIEF

One of two Deepstone swords with shoulder scabbard

Cybernetic eyepiece and cloth patch

NINJA FILE

LIKES: Stealing
DISLIKES: Losing bets
FRIENDS: Who needs friends when you can make money?
FOES: Everyone
SKILLS: Stealing, altering memories, piloting airships
GEAR: Stud shooters

SET NAME:
Ronin R.E.X.
SET NUMBER: 70735
YEAR: 2015

RONIN'S R.E.X.
Ronin is master of the skies in his awesome two-in-one airship. Equipped with an arsenal of weapons and a detachable Airjitzu flyer, Ronin is more than a match for the Ghost Warriors.

MOTIVATED BY GREED and money, the self-centred Ronin will do anyone's dirty work as long as he gets paid. Dressed in stolen samurai armor and wielding two guns and two swords, Ronin is smart and ruthless. This thief knows how to get his own way in any situation.

NINJA NYA

ELEMENTAL MASTER OF WATER

Two-layered zukin ninja headwrap

Sashes with new elemental water emblem

NYA'S AIRBIKE

This ninja has what it takes! Astride her sleek airbike, black hair blowing free in the wind, the Water Ninja can fend off the attacking ghouls, skillfully wielding her Deepstone katana and sai.

DID YOU KNOW?
Nya inherited the elemental power of water from her mother.

INTUITIVE NYA is back and is fulfilling her destiny! Under Master Wu's tutorship, Nya finds her inner ninja and learns to control her elemental power, water. Using hydrokinesis, this super warrior can manipulate and generate water, for a splash of serious girl power!

SOUL ARCHER

BOW MASTER

NINJA FILE

LIKES: Capturing souls
DISLIKES: Being cheated
FRIENDS: Morro
FOES: Shady Ronin
SKILLS: Turning enemies to ghosts with deadly arrows
GEAR: Bow and arrow

SET NAME: Master Wu Dragon, Final Flight of Destiny's Bounty
SET NUMBER: 70734, 70738
YEAR: 2015

Zukin-style ninja headwrap with purple knotted bandana

Shoulder pad armour with tattered robe draped over it

Trans-neon ghostly trail instead of leg piece

MORRO'S MAN

Soul Archer is Morro's right-hand man. Morro summoned him from the Cursed Realm for his arrow skills and nasty, no-nonsense nature to help him to get the Scrolls of Airjitzu.

THIS GRUESOME GHOUL is an awesome archer—no other ghost can hit a target like the Bow Master. He can create Skreemers by shooting his arrows. If these creatures attach themselves to a human's head, the human will turn into a ghost.

WRAYTH
CHAIN MASTER

Headpiece resembles a bandage-wrapped mummy, with black-shadowed eyes peeping out

DID YOU KNOW?
Wrayth and Soul Archer are two of four ghosts that don't have a transparent headpiece. The others are Wail and Pitch.

Tattered robe with heavy chain belts

Trans-neon leg piece so he can sit on his Chain Cycle

NINJA FILE

LIKES: Revving up his Chain Cycle
DISLIKES: Water
FRIENDS: Cowler
FOES: Unstoppable Kai
SKILLS: Catching souls with his cursed whip
GEAR: Chained whip

SET NAME: Chain Cycle Ambush, City of Stiix, Attack of the Morro Dragon, Airjitzu Wrayth Flyer
SET NUMBER: 70730, 70732, 70736, 70744
YEAR: 2015

GHOSTLY AIRJITZU FLYER
As well as his spine-chilling Chain Cycle with spiked wheels, Wrayth can spin through the air like a tornado on his ghostly neon Airjitzu flyer, to attack the ninja.

WRAYTH IS A WRAITH by nature and by name! This pale ghost has a haunting, cackling laugh and is one of Morro's trusted inner circle. Like his comrade, Soul Archer, Wraith can turn humans into ghosts by hitting them with his whip-like chain weapon.

BANSHA
BLADE MASTER

NINJA FILE

LIKES: Screaming
DISLIKES: Earplugs
FRIENDS: Ghost Warriors
FOES: Traitor Ronin
SKILLS: Telepathy, possession, killer scream
GEAR: Dual Ghost Master Blades

SET NAME: Jay Walker One, Titan Mech Battle, Final Flight of Destiny's Bounty
SET NUMBER: 70731, 70737, 70738
YEAR: 2015

Translucent neon female ghost headpiece

DID YOU KNOW?
Bansha's name and powers are a reference to the mythical Banshee, the wailing female spirit of folklore.

Beneath his armor, Bansha has red sleeves.

Tattered robe with leather strap holding a jagged-blade knife at the front and two shurikens at the back

GHOSTLY X MECH!
The Ghost Warriors possess Nya's Samurai X Mech and turn it into their own ghostly battle machine: Mech-enstein! With Bansha at the helm, they attack the ninja.

Trans-neon ghostly trail instead of leg piece

Hinged, posable legs and feet support the rotating Mech torso

WITH A WAILING, high-pitched scream that can shatter eardrums and cause avalanches, the Ghost Warrior Bansha is a terrifying and dangerous ethereal force. She can take over someone's body and mind from a distant location.

GHOULTAR
SCYTHE MASTER

Traditional bamboo conical hat

Bandana to cover lower face

Tattered robe with skeleton spine and ribs pattern showing through the torn material

NINJA FILE

LIKES: Dancing
DISLIKES: Getting trapped
FRIENDS: Bansha
FOES: Nya and Ronin
SKILLS: Strength—ghosts go to the gym too!
GEAR: Scythe Ghost Master Blade

SET NAME: City of Stiix, Ronin R.E.X., Titan Mech Battle, Final Flight of Destiny's Bounty
SET NUMBER: 70732, 70735, 70737, 70738
YEAR: 2015

DID YOU KNOW?
Ghoultar's exclusive head has white skull-shaped printing and detailing, unique to Ghoultar.

GHOSTBUSTERS!
Ghoultar's brute strength isn't enough to evade capture. Using a cage made of Deepstone, the ninja imprison the ghoul. And with the promise of his favorite Puffy Pot Stickers snack, Ghoultar is almost ready to talk!

WHAT GHOULTAR LACKS in brains, he makes up for in brute strength and his skills with the scythe. He's quick to follow orders and is a powerful warrior. Unfortunately Ghoultar has a destructive nature, and if he doesn't understand his orders he can bring disaster down on his own side!

HACKLER
UNDEAD GHOST NINJA

Tattered robes and regular ghost warrior standard armor

Trans-neon ghost leg piece

NINJA FILE

LIKES: Collecting weapons of all shapes and sizes
DISLIKES: Blunt blades
FRIENDS: Pitch
FOES: Zane
SKILLS: Blocking attacks with his super-tough shield
GEAR: Ghost Ax Blade

SET NAME: Master Wu Dragon
SET NUMBER: 70734
YEAR: 2015

GHOST WEAPONS

The Ghost Warriors have an arsenal of weapons at their disposal—swords, axes, daggers, and scythes. Armed with his Ax Blade, Hackler loves to use his favorite ghost weapon against the enemy down in combat!

HACKLER JOINS MORRO'S motley ghoul crew as another terrifying henchman when he is summoned from the Cursed Realm. With the stealth and cunning of a ninja and his excellent weapon skills, this ghostly warrior is an asset to the Ghost Army. Watch out, ninja!

Hackler uses his shield to fend off his enemies.

ATTILA
GHOSTLY, BUT GRACEFUL

Translucent neon ghost headpiece with bushy eyebrows

Regular Ghost warrior standard armor

Ghost katana is Attila's favorite weapon

NINJA FILE

LIKES: Giving that troublesome Ronin a good fright
DISLIKES: Aeroblades
FRIENDS: Hackler
FOES: Jay
SKILLS: Ravaging enemies
GEAR: Ghost katana

SET NAME: Ronin R.E.X.
SET NUMBER: 70735
YEAR: 2015

GHOST DRAGON
The Ghost Warriors sometimes use dragons as a mode of speedy transportation or as an aid in battle. Ghost Dragons do not have limbs (except Morro's), so swoop through the air using their ethereal bodies and whip-like tails.

A FEARLESS WARRIOR, this Ghost Ninja is one of a kind. He has the grace and agility of a ninja, dodging blows in combat swiftly and with ease. Attila moves silently and smoothly through the air—the perfect skill for sneaking up on his foes.

SPYDER
NO ARACHNOPHOBE

Ghost saber, Spyder's weapon of choice

Giant neon decorative spider emblem

DID YOU KNOW?

Spyder's haunting melody is soft and eerie and seems to come from everywhere, making it hard to track him down.

SPOOKY AERIAL DUEL

Morro and his evil ghost minions launch a terrifying attack on the ninja on board their airship, *Destiny's Bounty*. Can the ninja withstand this deadly onslaught and avoid being possessed?

AS HIS NAME SUGGESTS, Spyder has an obsession with eight-legged creatures. As well as being a superb warrior, this warbling Ghost Ninja also has the power to send shivers up the spine of even the bravest of opponents with his spooky singing voice!

MING

GETTING IDEAS ABOVE HIS STATION

DID YOU KNOW?

Ming takes his work very seriously and he has no patience for ghosts who think everything is fun and frights!

Pointed headwrap with ghostly trans-neon cloth at the back

Trans-neon leg piece with robe sash detail

Ghost Energy Blade

NINJA FILE

LIKES: Glowing green
DISLIKES: Stud shooters
FRIENDS: Cyrus
FOES: Nya, the Water Ninja
SKILLS: Flipping his blade
GEAR: Ghost Energy Blade

SET NAME: City of Stiix
SET NUMBER: 70732
YEAR: 2015

STIIX AND STONES

When the ninja go to Stiix to find Ronin and the Scrolls of Airjitzu, Morro brings his warriors to the spooky city to ambush them. Employing his superior fighting skills, Ming leads the charge!

CLEVER AND SCARY, Ming is something of an expert on fighting techniques. The other ghosts come to him to get tips on how to fight and win outside of the Cursed Realm. Ming trains hard and he is always trying to better himself. He may look the same as his fellow Ghost Ninja, but he feels very different.

CYRUS

FIGHTING PHANTOM

Traditional conical hat denotes lower rank in Ghost Army.

Crossbow is Cyrus's weapon of choice

Variant ghost armor from standard Ghost Army issue

DID YOU KNOW?

Cyrus only fights for Morro because he's bored and has nothing better to do. Sometimes being a ghost is no fun!

ALL ABOARD, SHIPMATES!

Ghosts are not natural seafarers – water and ghosts don't mix. But some ghoul has to man the boat if they are to follow the ninja to Stiix. Let's hope they don't have to walk the plank!

SNEAKY AND IRRITATING, Cyrus doesn't have many ghostly friends, if any! He doesn't really care about Morro's evil plans. Just as well he's an excellent fighter—it's the only reason Morro keeps him in his army. He is decked out accordingly as a soldier.

PITCH
FUN-SEEKING GHOST WARRIOR

NINJA FILE

LIKES: Poking ninja with his fork
DISLIKES: Cyrus's jokes
FRIENDS: Attila
FOES: Cole
SKILLS: Swift stabbing
GEAR: Pitchfork, dagger

SET NAME: Master Wu Dragon
SET NUMBER: 70734
YEAR: 2015

DID YOU KNOW?
All ghosts except Yokai are scared of water. A bucketful is enough to dispense these evil spirits in a puff of ghostly vapor!

Basket—useful for holding ghost discs, rocks for throwing at the enemy and food (of course!)

Dagger—Pitch's weapon of choice

Pitchfork—useful as a weapon or for just poking things (especially ninja!) for fun

UNDERCOVER SPOOKS
If he wants to sneak into Master Wu's tea farm to attack the ninja, what should a ghost do? Possess a rickshaw and install a hidden disc shooter in it, of course!

WORK IS THE LAST THING on Pitch's childish mind. He may be a grown-up in spirit but at heart he's just a big kid. He'd rather be playing games or out haunting houses just for the fun of it, than fighting! Pitch's all-black face makes him a pair with Wail.

COWLER
IMITATION ARTIST

Two ghost katanas held in back scabbard

Ghost Blade Spear

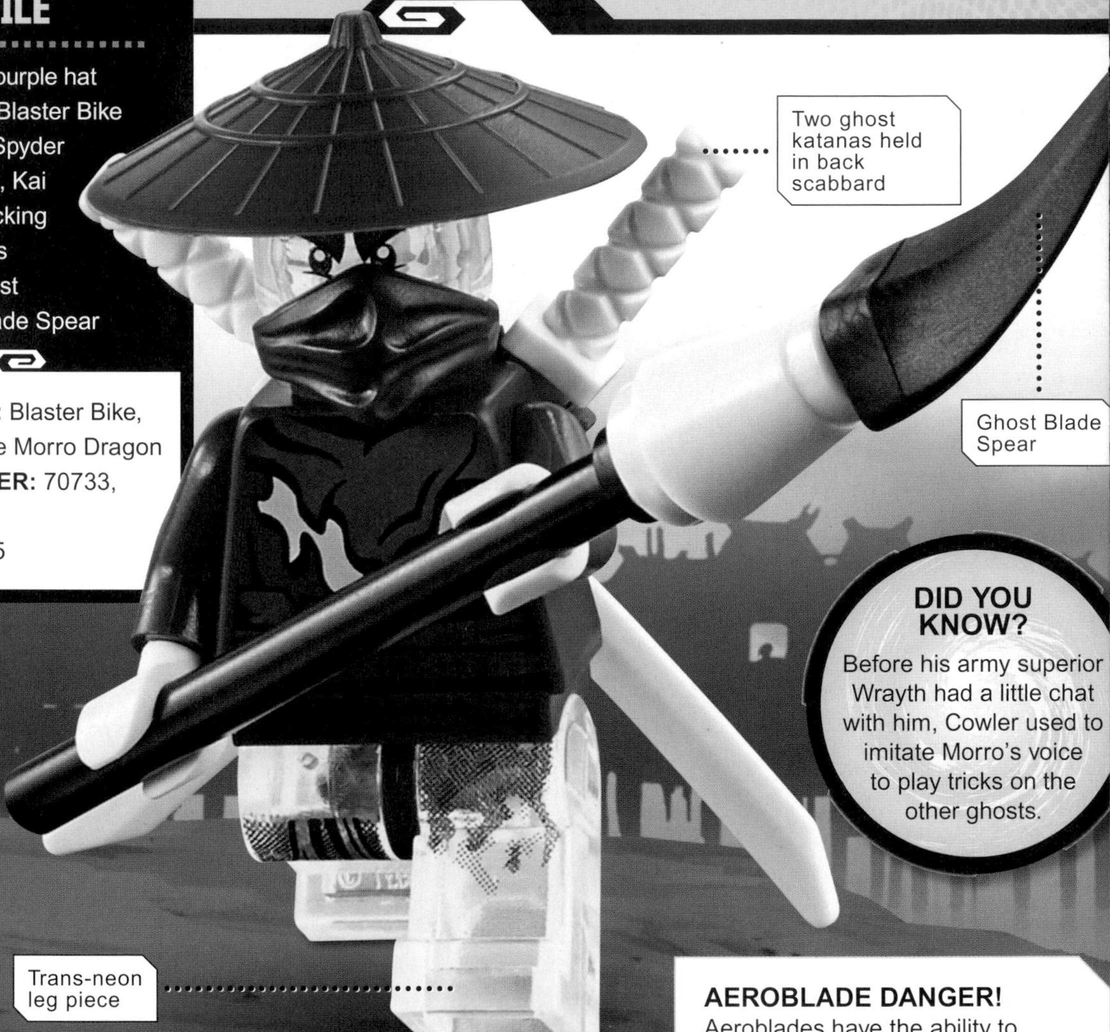

DID YOU KNOW?
Before his army superior Wrayth had a little chat with him, Cowler used to imitate Morro's voice to play tricks on the other ghosts.

Trans-neon leg piece

AEROBLADE DANGER!
Aeroblades have the ability to defeat ghosts. Glowing red with his elemental fire power, Kai is ready to use the shuriken-like weapon against Cowler. But can he dodge the ghost's Blade Spear?

COWLER TAKES HIS scaring seriously—the more frightened he can make someone, the better! Otherwise, what's the point of being a ghost? His favorite trick is to imitate the voice of someone's best friend to lure them into a trap!

WAIL
SILENT AS THE GRAVE

NINJA FILE

LIKES: Stillness
DISLIKES: Critics
FRIENDS: Cyrus
FOES: Jay
SKILLS: Ambushes
GEAR: Ghost Ninja Kamas

SET NAME: Jay Walker One
SET NUMBER: 70731
YEAR: 2015

Ghost Ninja Kamas—two are definitely better than one!

DID YOU KNOW?
Wail is an expert warrior and mostly wins his battles. Just as well, because Morro finds his ambush addiction very annoying!

HAUNTED PORTAL
The ninja must dodge flying ghost discs and seize the Aeroblade magically suspended in the haunted temple gateway, before the evil Ghost Warriors turn them into ghosts, too.

WAIL BY NAME, but not by nature! Oddly enough, this sinister ghoul never makes a sound. Wail loves the thrill of the ambush, and silence and stealth are essential for this. Wail will postpone a battle for an hour or two, just so he can surprise his opponent by leaping out of the shadows!

GHURKA

GLUM GHOST WARRIOR

NINJA FILE

LIKES: Showing off his archery skills
DISLIKES: Distractions
FRIENDS: Wail
FOES: Jay
SKILLS: Flawless aim
GEAR: Crossbow and quiver

SET NAME: Jay Walker One
SET NUMBER: 70731
YEAR: 2015

Lurid green hands

Quiver of arrows for crossbow

Crossbow is the perfect weapon for a marksman.

DID YOU KNOW?

Because of his fear of ghosts, Ghurka often goes into battle with his eyes shut! Remarkably, he rarely misses his target with his crossbow!

SUPER ARCHER!

Ghurka is the second-best archer in Morro's army. He can hit a bullseye, even with his eyes shut! He strikes fast, launching a steady stream of arrows before vanishing into thin air.

GHURKA IS AN EXPERT marksman and a powerful warrior. However, he has one big weakness: phasmophobia—the fear of ghosts! He can't bring himself to look at other members of the Ghost Army, so Morro often sends Ghurka into combat as a one-spirit squad.

YOKAI
WATER-LOVING WARRIOR

Double-ended spiked spear staff

Ripped robe, common to many Ghost Army members

GHOSTLY SKREEMERS!
Beware the wispy, screeching, green creatures created by the Soul Archer's arrows. If they attach themselves to a human's head, the human will turn into a ghost. Always hungry, Skreemers love munching on snacks.

LIKE HIS FELLOW ghosts-in-arms, Yokai is an excellent warrior and a dangerous force when he is wielding his spiked spear. However, whereas most ghosts are afraid of water, Yokai isn't. He loves being near water, although sadly he can't actually go swimming in the wet stuff!

OW TO FIGHT A GHOST ARMY:

MASTER ANCIENT ARTS, SUCH AS AIRJITZU

TURN ADVERSITY INTO ADVANTAGE

IMPROVIZE ATTACKS WITH NEW WEAPONS

ACQUIRE NEW POWERS TO OUTSMART YOUR FOES

::IRJITZU K::I

SPINNING FIRE FLYER

New ninja robe with
flame pattern and
Kai's elemental symbol
on the front and his
fire emblem on the
back of the torso.

SPINJITZU TO AIRJITZU

Airjitzu is an extension of the
martial arts technique of Spinjitzu.
By tapping deeper into his
elemental energy Kai is able to
create an airborne vortex of fire.

Blade of Wildfire—this
triple-action weapon
encompasses two scyth
blades (one spiked, the
other jagged) and a
burning fire sword.

BY LEARNING THE ANCIENT ART of Airjitzu,
Kai has reached a higher level of his true ninja
potential. His new flame-patterned robe reflects
this elevated status. Focusing on the power of his
fire energy, Kai creates a tornado-like vortex
around himself and levitates over the land. Maybe
now the ninja will be a match for the ghosts.

AIRJITZU JAY

SPINNING LIGHTNING FLYER

Unique blue headpiece with lightning patterns around the eyes

Electro torch

NINJA FILE

LIKES: Cyclondo
DISLIKES: Temple traps where they're learning Airjitzu
FRIENDS: Misako, ninja
FOES: Ghastly Morro
SKILLS: Using technology
GEAR: Thunder Head

SET NAME: Airjitzu Jay Flyer
SET NUMBER: 70740
YEAR: 2015

MASTER OF AIRJITZU
Ghost Master Yang was the creator of the martial art form Airjitzu. He left a scroll on which he wrote down the techniques of this ancient art.

DID YOU KNOW?
Jay decides to call the martial arts technique of Airjitzu "Cyclondo" because he thinks it sounds cooler!

AT FIRST, the Master of Lightning struggles to focus his mind on creating enough energy to make his Airjitzu tornado. However, when Master Wu offers him wise and encouraging words, Jay finally finds his groove. The sparks fly and Jay spins up into the air at lightning speed!

::IRJITZU COL::

SPINNING EARTH FLYER

NINJA FILE

LIKES: Airjitzu weapons
DISLIKES: Turning into a ghost
FRIENDS: Nya
FOES: Wrayth
SKILLS: Vanishing at will
GEAR: Cleaver

SET NAME: Airjitzu Cole Flyer
SET NUMBER: 70741
YEAR: 2015

Ninja robe with broken rock pattern

Double-headed Cleaver with two scythe-like blades

Broken rock pattern continues onto legs

THE HAUNTED TEMPLE

Cole makes the ultimate sacrifice for his friends. It is when he goes back into the Temple of Airjitzu to retrieve the scroll revealing the secret techniques of this powerful ancient art that he is turned into a ghost.

COLE IS NOT HAPPY about recent events—he has been turned into a ghost! Before he can achieve the correct state of mind needed for Airjitzu, he must reconquer his fears and come to terms with his new ghost form. With a lot of reassurance from his friends, Cole is able to channel his earth element.

AIRJITZU ZANE

SPINNING ICE FLYER

NINJA FILE

LIKES: Cryokinesis
DISLIKES: Speaking in strange dialects
FRIENDS: Jay
FOES: Flies! They're a technology hazard.
SKILLS: Storing data
GEAR: Polearm

SET NAME: Airjitzu Zane Flyer
SET NUMBER: 70742
YEAR: 2015

Polearm Ice Sword with added jagged scythe blade

Ninja robe with ice shard pattern

ICE VORTEX

Airjitzu grants the user the ability to fly in a small elemental vortex for a limited time. Zane propels himself upwards using the power and energy of his element, ice.

ONE ADVANTAGE OF being a Nindroid is having a superior machine mind. Zane applies his computer logic to learning the art of Airjitzu. Before long, the cool ninja is combining his powers and channelling his freezing energies to rocket into the sky in an awesome icy tornado.

TEMPLE WU
TEA EXPERT

NINJA FILE
....

LIKES: Serving tea
DISLIKES: Coffee
FRIENDS: Misako
FOES: The Preeminent
SKILLS: Giving advice
GEAR: Teapot. It only appears harmless.

SET NAME: Temple of Airjitzu
SET NUMBER: 70751
YEAR: 2015

DID YOU KNOW?
The ninja have shares in Wu's tea shop. Kai gives this money to Ronin in order to save his life.

Long, gold sleeveless vest over robe with golden flower symbol on back of torso

Elaborate design continues on to legs

"T" FOR TRANQUILI-TEA
Wu couldn't think of a more idyllic way to spend his retirement than making and drinking his favorite hot beverage! While the tea brews, the old Spinjitzu Master offers his customers words of wisdom.

AFTER MANY YEARS of mentoring and teaching, the ever-patient Wu is happy to hang up his fighting robes. His stylish long vest and gi are perfect for relaxing in the new tea shop he runs with Misako. Retirement seems to be suiting Wu well, but will he be allowed to enjoy a simpler life for long?

MISAKO
ARCHEOLOGIST

Gray hair piece comes with a long French braided ponytail

Dual-sided head: one face with glasses, smile, and laughter lines; one with an amused expression

Safari-style suit with pockets, green neck bandana, and leather belt

NINJA FILE

LIKES: Painting
DISLIKES: Interruptions—an artist needs her space
FRIENDS: Wu
FOES: Ghosts and ghouls
SKILLS: Guiding ninja against ghosts
GEAR: Paintbrush

SET NAME: Temple of Airjitzu
SET NUMBER: 70751
YEAR: 2015

HIDDEN TALENT

Misako is a keen painter. When she's not researching history, helping Wu teach the ninja, or working in the tea shop, Misako relaxes by taking up her brush and putting paint to canvas. The Temple of Airjitzu set comes complete with an artist's studio.

ARTISTIC MISAKO works at the Ninjago Museum of History as an archaeologist and researcher. When the ninja go to Ninjago City to face the Stone Army, they meet Misako and discover that she is actually Lloyd's mother and Garmadon's long-lost wife.

NINJAGO MAILMAN

EXPRESS DELIVERY

NINJA FILE

LIKES: Delivering mail
DISLIKES: Climbing steps
FRIENDS: Pen pals
FOES: E-mail users
SKILLS: Alarming ninja by ringing the bell in the middle of an attack.
GEAR: Stylish satchel

SET NAME: Temple of Airjitzu
SET NUMBER: 70751
YEAR: 2015

DID YOU KNOW?
The mailman is a recurring background character in the NINJAGO™ TV series, but appears for the first time as a minifigure in the Temple of Airjitzu set.

Purple jacket features mail horn logo.

Letter tile with an elaborate signature

WELCOME BREAK
In the Temple of Airjitzu, the mailman is one of the many guests who enjoy watching a shadow puppet show. He sits alongside the ninja, Claire, and Jesper.

TRULY DEDICATED TO HIS JOB, the mailman goes beyond the call of duty to deliver mail to the ninja. No mountain is too high, no terrain too dangerous or bizarre, and no hideout too secret for this tireless postal hero. By air or by sea, no delivery is too distant. He is definitely a first-class chap!

DARETH
MASTER OF CHARM

NINJA FILE

LIKES: Bragging
DISLIKES: Messing up his hair
FRIENDS: Jesper
FOES: Ghosts
SKILLS: Charming others
GEAR: Shovel

SET NAME: Temple of Airjitzu
SET NUMBER: 70751
YEAR: 2015

DID YOU KNOW?
Before he became an instructor, Dareth toured Ninjago Island as a singer with a show named "Brown Suede Shoes."

Standard LEGO shovel can be used as a weapon.

New ninja robes with star pendant and star emblem on back of torso, and elaborate gold trim

LOYAL FRIEND
Dareth is always ready to go the extra mile for his ninja friends. He might not be able to protect them in a battle, but he can cook them a feast from food found in the Temple of Airjitzu and entertain them with his embellished stories!

IN SPITE OF his constant bragging and belief that he is a "legend," Dareth is a likeable guy and a loyal friend to the ninja. What he lacks in real ninja skills, he makes up for with his creative flair and his smooth charm. However, his new robes reveal he hasn't given up his obsession with medals!

JESPER

TEMPLE GROUNDSMAN

DID YOU KNOW?
Jesper first came across the ninja when he was fishing in the river by the ancient Temple of Airjitzu.

Catch of the day!

Outback-style cowboy hat worn with neck bandana

NINJA FILE

LIKES: A tidy temple
DISLIKES: Dirty ponds
FRIENDS: Funny Dareth
FOES: Ghosts
SKILLS: Fishing
GEAR: Fishing rod, and sometimes a fish

SET NAME: Temple of Airjitzu
SET NUMBER: 70751
YEAR: 2015

Casual safari-style shirt with smiley face badge on pocket

Protective apron covered in stains

FISHERMAN'S FRIEND
Jesper is a good friend of Dareth's. The competitive fishing pals can never agree on who has caught the biggest fish!

BEARDED JESPER spends his days keeping the Temple of Airjitzu shiny and clean. In his spare time he enjoys searching for the best fishing spots on Ninjago Island and trying to catch the biggest fish ever. His minifigure is kitted out accordingly, and well suited for the great outdoors.

CLAIRE
JESPER'S DAUGHTER

Claire always carries her brush with her—it makes a handy weapon!

This amulet-style necklace might bring good luck and ward off ghosts!

DID YOU KNOW?

Claire does not actually appear in the NINJAGO™ TV series, although her minifigure is included in the Temple of Airjitzu set.

BATWING GLIDER

Thrill-seeker Claire can hardly contain her excitement when she gets to take the Batwing Glider for a spin around the temple, especially as she gets to meet the adventurous ninja.

JESPER'S DAUGHTER, CLAIRE, has always thought that her dad's job—looking after the Temple of Airjitzu grounds—was pretty boring. But she gets a fright when she becomes embroiled in the ninja's latest adventure. Skreemers and weapon-wielding ghosts are the stuff of nightmares!

AT THE TEMPLE OF AIRJITZU :

ENJOY A SHADOW PUPPET SHOW

RELAX WITH MASTER WU AND A CUP OF TEA

GO FISHING ALONGSIDE DARETH

LEARN ABOUT THE TEMPLE'S HAUNTED HISTORY

IN THE SIXTH SEASON of NINJAGO™: Masters of Spinjitzu the ninja are superstars—appearing in their own TV show and adored by fans. But danger is looming, with the escape of notorious djinn Nadakhan, and his rowdy crew—the Sky Pirates! With an evil djinn on the scene, the ninja must be careful of what they wish for... A total of seven sets bring the battle to life!

MAKE A WISH, NINJA. I DARE YOU!

I DON'T NEED ANY WISHES TO DEFEAT YOU!

LLOYD
MASTER-IN-TRAINING

Golden weapon staff

Ornate cloth belt tie ends with golden clasps.

Dragon symbol on new robes is unique to Lloyd.

DID YOU KNOW?

Lloyd is not comfortable with the ninja's new celebrity status. He will not let anything get in the way of being a hero.

SOARING AHEAD

With a new dark force conspiring to ruin Ninjago Island, Lloyd's focus is on the tasks ahead. With this fire-blasting jetpack he is ready for any magical threats coming from the skies above.

Flames made from transparent LEGO pieces

LLOYD GARMADON is firmly committed to his ninja duties and never forgets his reason for being or the purpose of his powers. Fully focused, and wearing robes that mean business, the Green Ninja is ready to train with Wu to become a Master himself.

COLE
LIVING GHOST

Face now a ghostly green color

NINJA FILE

LIKES: Pulling Jay's leg
DISLIKES: Thermal vision
FRIENDS: Serious Lloyd
FOES: Dogshank
SKILLS: Quick thinking
GEAR: Katanas, scythe

SET NAME: Cole's Dragon, Tiger Widow Island
SET NUMBER: 70599, 70604
YEAR: 2016

DID YOU KNOW?

As a ghost, Cole has had to learn how to make physical contact with objects and how to move through walls.

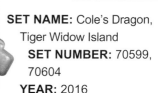

Silver arms match head wrap and belt tie.

GHOST DRAGON RIDER

Even as a ghost, Cole is an awesome ninja. With Master Wu's guidance, he has learnt to control his elemental earth powers, and can call upon his ghost dragon in battle. This new beast is small but snappy!

WITH THE HELP of his friends and Wu, Cole is learning to accept his new living ghost form. The journey has not been easy, but Cole has tapped into his true ninja essence and confronted his despair and fears. He is now ready to face the new ghostly challenges ahead of him.

ZANE
NINDROID BROTHER-IN-ARMS

NINJA FILE

LIKES: Mini-droid chess
DISLIKES: Hackers who invade his system
FRIENDS: Jay
FOES: Fickle Ronin
SKILLS: Logical thinking
GEAR: Golden katanas

SET NAME: Raid Zeppelin
SET NUMBER: 70603
YEAR: 2016

Zane's rebuilt Nindroid headpiece with cybernetic eye

Single pauldron allows for freer movement in battle.

New Skybound ninja robe shows a whirlwind-style emblem representing Zane's elemental ice powers.

A pair of katanas can still be slotted into the ninja's new back piece.

ICY FLYER
Sitting at the controls of his super cool shuriken-style hover battle machine, Zane calculates the right moment to strike, and then speedily and stealthily zooms up on his enemies.

FULLY REBOOTED and functioning at maximum Nindroid capacity, Zane is glad to be back with his team, training and refining his ninja skills. Being a Nindroid, Zane's not really fazed by the group's sudden celebrity—he'd rather be computing his battle strategies!

KAI

RED-HOT CELEBRITY!

LIKES: Gushing fangirls
DISLIKES: Serving prison time in Kryptarium
FRIENDS: Cole
FOES: Sqiffy
SKILLS: Pulling a ruse
GEAR: Golden katanas

SET NAME: Ninja Bike Chase, Misfortune's Keep
SET NUMBER: 70600, 70605
YEAR: 2016

Two-tone colored head wrap

DID YOU KNOW?

Now that the team has achieved celebrity status, action figure toys of each of the ninja have hit the stores across Ninjago Island!

Three clasps fasten the side of the new Skybound robes.

SUPER BIKE

This magnificent bike with its all-terrain giant wheels is certainly fit for a celeb! Whether cruising round town waving to adoring fans, or chasing evil Sky Pirates, Kai has the skills to handle this awesome ninja machine.

Ornate knee-ties secure robes.

LOOK FOR THE CROWDS of adoring fans and the Master of Fire is sure to be at the center of all the attention. Kai loves being a celebrity. Let's hope that with his famous hot temper, he doesn't become a ninja diva, or he might forget what his real job is!

JAY

HEROIC NINJA

NINJA FILE

LIKES: Helping his ninja friends

DISLIKES: Making a wish!

FRIENDS: Zane

FOES: Nadakhan

SKILLS: Saving his friends

GEAR: Golden katanas

SET NAME: Jay's Elemental Dragon, Misfortune's Keep

SET NUMBER: 70602, 70605

YEAR: 2016

Jay's regular face peeks out from beneath this side of his head wrap.

DID YOU KNOW?

Jay has discovered that he was adopted and that his true father was a famous actor, and also his movie idol!

Like those of his fellow ninja, Jay's outfit is accessorised with black gi and gloves.

SHIVER ME TIMBERS!

When the evil Nadakhan and his fearsome band of Sky Pirates kidnap Jay, he craftily disguises himself as one of the brigands to try and make his escape before they force him to walk the plank.

Eye patch over one eye completes Jay's disguise.

CREATIVE JAY enjoys solving problems. But when it comes to love, none of Jay's inventions can fix his heartbreak. When Nya tells Jay that she only wants to be friends with him, the distraught ninja is tempted by the evil djinn's dark wishes. However, he soon discovers that you can't wish for love.

JAY'S DRAGON

HYDRO-ELECTRIC BEAST

NINJA FILE

LIKES: Mixing things up
DISLIKES: Pirates
FRIENDS: Jay, Nya
FOES: Cyren
SKILLS: Coming up
with contingency plans
GEAR: Golden sai

SET NAME: Jay's
Elemental Dragon
SET NUMBER:
70602
YEAR: 2016

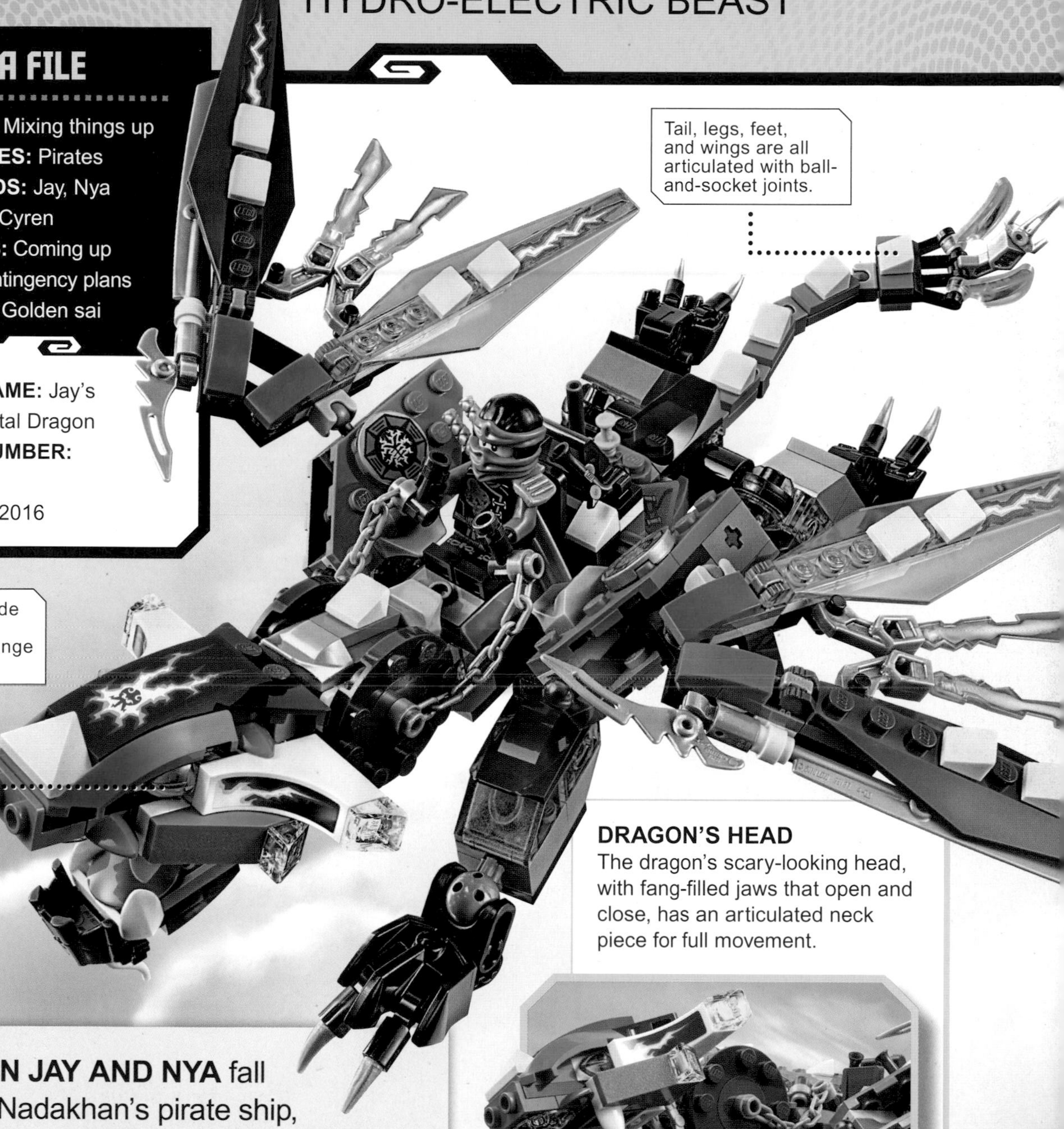

Tail, legs, feet, and wings are all articulated with ball-and-socket joints.

Eyes made from trans-orange bricks

DRAGON'S HEAD

The dragon's scary-looking head, with fang-filled jaws that open and close, has an articulated neck piece for full movement.

WHEN JAY AND NYA fall from Nadakhan's pirate ship, *Misfortune's Keep*, the two ninja combine their elemental powers—water and lightning—to create this dragon. The resulting creature sizzles with lightning bolts and water power.

NYA

INDEPENDENT NINJA

Deep red color is iconic to Nya.

New emblem in the blue colour of Nya's water element decorates her robes.

NINJA FILE

LIKES: Being part of a team
DISLIKES: Not being taken seriously
FRIENDS: Master Wu
FOES: Dogshank
SKILLS: Fighting Sky Pirates
GEAR: Golden katanas

SET NAME: Ninja Bike Chase, Jay's Elemental Dragon, Tiger Widow Island
SET NUMBER: 70600, 70602, 70604
YEAR: 2016

MISSION POSSIBLE

Without his Djinn Blade, Nadakhan is not so powerful. If Nya and Wu can steal the magical weapon, they just might be able to save the spirits trapped inside it.

AFTER MONTHS of intense training with Wu, Nya is now a fully-fledged Master of Water and part of the team. But she is fed up with all of the attention that the boys get and wants to be recognized for her skills in her own right. Time for Nya to strike out on her own!

STONE WARRIOR JAY

EXCLUSIVE ARMOR

DID YOU KNOW?

The Stone Warrior armor was first seen in Episode 34, *The Titanium Ninja*, of the NINJAGO™: Masters of Spinjitzu TV series.

Fabric straps join with metal armour in the centre of Jay's torso.

Two silver katanas are held in Jay's back pauldrons.

NINJA FILE

LIKES: Reading comics

DISLIKES: Days when the comic-book store is closed

FRIENDS: Stone Warrior ninja

FOES: Nindroids

SKILLS: Speed-reading

GEAR: Silver katanas

SET NAME: DK's LEGO® NINJAGO™ *Character Encyclopedia: Updated and Expanded*

YEAR: 2016

STARFARER

Jay's favourite comic, *Starfarer*, is represented in a simple LEGO tile. Jay idolises the action hero who stars on its pages, and it might be Jay's destiny to share more than just a love of adventure with the famous Fritz Donnegan!

WEARING HIS Stone Warrior armor, Jay is ready to embark on adventures and emulate his favourite action hero—Fritz Donnegan. In this solid silver armor, Jay can take on any foe, and can join Lloyd, Zane and Kai, who have appeared in minifigure form in this armor, too.

WELCOME TO DJINJAGO!

NOTORIOUS BY NATURE, DJINNS TWIST THE WORDS OF EVERY WISH

HOME TO DJINNS, WHO HAVE THE POWER TO GRANT WISHES

NOTORIOUS BY NATURE, DJINNS TWIST THE WORDS OF EVERY WISH

THEY FULFILL THE WISH BUT DO SO BY RUINING SOMETHING ELSE

NADAKHAN

CAPTAIN OF THE SKY PIRATES

NINJA FILE

LIKES: Breaking apart Ninjago Island

DISLIKES: Failing his father

FRIENDS: Sky Pirates

FOES: Ninja

SKILLS: Granting wishes

GEAR: Djinn Blade

SET NAME: Misfortune's Keep

SET NUMBER: 70605

YEAR: 2016

Genie-style hairpiece

Sky Pirate skull-and-crossbones emblem

Extra torso incorporates two extra arms.

Studded belt to match armour

Standard LEGO pirate hook hand

Transparent orange genie tail

TRANSFORMATIVE POWERS

Monkey Wretch was once a skilled human ship mechanic, before Nadakhan tricked him into wishing for more hands and more speed, and turned him into a mechanical monkey. Wretch does all the general repairs on Nadakhan's ship, *Misfortune's Keep*.

NADAKHAN, PRINCE OF DJINJAGO, is a djinn, a magical being who can grant wishes. He blames the ninja for the destruction of his homeland, Djinjago, and with his motley pirate crew in tow, he is now seeking revenge.

CLANCEE
SERPENTINE SKY PIRATE

Serpentine snake head with fangs

Padded shoulder pauldrons

NINJA FILE

LIKES: Swabbing the deck
DISLIKES: Heights, the sea
FRIENDS: Still looking
FOES: All of Captain
Nadakhan's enemies
SKILLS: Evading traps
GEAR: Mop

SET NAME: Raid Zeppelin
SET NUMBER: 70603
YEAR: 2016

DID YOU KNOW?
Poor Clancee gets seasick and airsick—not great when you're a pirate sailing the high seas or whizzing through the air on a flying boat!

Rusty body armor and strap with ragged shirt displaying Sky Pirate emblem

Simple, brown wooden peg leg

WISHFUL THINKING
Clancee may not be the brightest crew member, but he knows Nadakhan is not to be trusted. By not asking for a wish, Clancee has probably, without even knowing it, saved his own scaly skin!

HOW THIS nervous Serpentine ended up as part of the crew on *Misfortune's Keep* is anyone's guess, but peg-legged Clancee is content to live the life of a pirate, even though he gets the worst jobs. He is often found mopping down the decks and cleaning up after his shipmates.

FLINTLOCKE

SKY PIRATE FIRST MATE

Pilot goggles worn on top of green flying helmet

Separate bushy mustache piece

NINJA FILE

LIKES: His Sky Shark
DISLIKES: Secrets
FRIENDS: Nadakhan
FOES: Lloyd
SKILLS: Inspiring his crew to charge into battle
GEAR: Pistols

SET NAME: Sky Shark, Misfortune's Keep
SET NUMBER: 70601, 70605
YEAR: 2016

Flintlocke wields two pirate pistols at once.

DID YOU KNOW?

Flintlocke pilots the sleek Sky Shark jet, which serves as an advance scout for the *Misfortune's Keep*.

SKY SHARK

With Flintlocke at the helm, this battle jet searches the skies for enemy aircraft. It then slices through sail and steel with its anchor-shaped wings, before the *Misfortune's Keep* arrives.

Mismatched legs (one brown, one orange), covered in armor plating, straps and buckles.

FLINTLOCKE is Nadakhan's trusted right-hand man. He's loyal to his djinn captain and will follow him anywhere—as long as he knows where they're heading. But if he's expecting his leader to return his loyalty, then he's on the wrong ship!

Hidden dynamite drop function

DOGSHANK

HULKING SKY PIRATE

Horned helmet comes complete with built-in mouth visor, spiked pauldron, and skull emblem.

NINJA FILE

LIKES: Fair fights
DISLIKES: Flintlocke's jokes
FRIENDS: Monkey Wretch
FOES: Nya
SKILLS: Twirling her anchor dangerously on a chain
GEAR: Ship's anchor

SET NAME: Tiger Widow Island
SET NUMBER: 70604
YEAR: 2016

Oversized bigfig hands can clutch weapons.

ON TIGER WIDOW ISLAND

Will Nya's stealthy ninja battle skills be enough to combat the brute strength and size of Dogshank? The pirate swings her weapon of choice, an anchor and chain, at the Master of Water as they fight.

BELIEVE IT OR NOT, this hulking brute was once a woman of normal size! She made the mistake of making a wish with Nadakhan—and this new shape and size was the result! Dogshank is now a large and dangerous foe for the ninja.

DOUBLOON
SILENCED THIEF

NINJA FILE

LIKES: Masks
DISLIKES: Talking
FRIENDS: Sqiffy
FOES: Jay
SKILLS: Spinjitzu
GEAR: Pirate swords

SET NAME: Raid Zeppelin
SET NUMBER: 70603
YEAR: 2016

Horns top Doubloon's samurai-style helmet.

Long fangs curl in sinister fashion up the sides of Doubloon's face.

Red face markings add sinister element

Doubloon, Cyren and Bucko have the same chest armour printed on their torsos

RAID ZEPPELIN
Behind the wheel of his Raid Zepplin, the silent Doubloon fires the bow-mounted cannon at the enemy. The mid-sized ship, held aloft by gas bags filled with hot air, is one of the Sky Pirates' most potent weapons.

DOUBLOON WAS ONCE a two-faced, double-crossing thief who tried to steal gold from Nadakhan, and now he is physically two-faced for eternity. The treacherous pirate has two permanent masks stuck to his head—one with a happy fang-filled grin, and the other an unhappy grimace.

SQIFFY
SMELLY SKY PIRATE

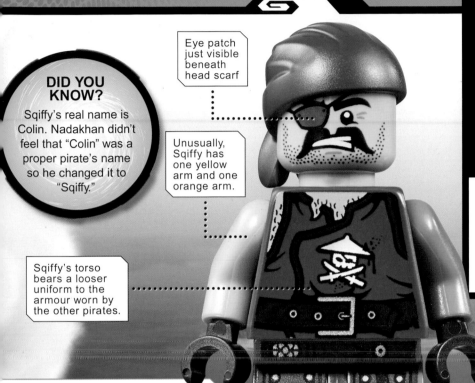

Eye patch just visible beneath head scarf

DID YOU KNOW?
Sqiffy's real name is Colin. Nadakhan didn't feel that "Colin" was a proper pirate's name so he changed it to "Sqiffy."

Unusually, Sqiffy has one yellow arm and one orange arm.

Sqiffy's torso bears a looser uniform to the armour worn by the other pirates.

NINJA FILE

LIKES: Fierce pirate names
DISLIKES: Being the new guy in the crew
FRIENDS: Flintlocke, Doubloon
FOES: Kai
SKILLS: Pestering ninja
GEAR: Pirate sword

SET NAME: Ninja Bike Chase, Ninja Island
SET NUMBER: 70600, 70604
YEAR: 2016

Sqiffy sports identical legs to Doubloon and Cyren, but the opposite way round to Flintlocke and Bucko.

SKY GLIDER
Armed with weapons and designed for quick turns and rapid ascent, these pirate gliders have enough power to bring down a bigger vessel. Sqiffy skillfully flies it to team up with other pirate gliders—together they can launch a more effective raid on the enemy.

EVERYONE KNOWS THAT pirates don't wash, and Sqiffy is no exception! This colourful character is the stinkiest pirate around. The unshaven new recruit is eager to show the captain his awesome sword skills, and what a frightening pirate he is—not just in terms of smell.

CYREN
SINGING SKY PIRATE

NINJA FILE

LIKES: Applause
DISLIKES: Missing an opportunity to sing
FRIENDS: Bucko
FOES: Cole
SKILLS: Sending people into a trance with her singing
GEAR: Serrated sword

SET NAME: Jay Dragon
SET NUMBER: 70602
YEAR: 2016

Headpiece shows angry facial expression, with a beauty spot and eye patch.

Two belts cross standard Sky Pirate torso.

Standard-issue brown pirate gloves

SINGING RAIDS

Cyren can't perform on stage any more, but she can use her secret weapon on a glider raid. One quick tune and the enemy is brought to their knees. She deserves some applause for that party trick!

CYREN IS ANOTHER VICTIM of one of Nadakhan's twisted wishes. She wanted to be the greatest singer in the world, but instead, the Djinn made her voice capable of temporarily sending humans into a catatonic trance. Not a great career move!

BUCKO
IT'S A PIRATE'S LIFE FOR HIM

NINJA FILE

LIKES: The Raid Zeppelin
DISLIKES: Being bullied
by fellow pirates
FRIENDS: Doubloon
FOES: Cole
SKILLS: Growling fiercely
GEAR: Djinn Blade

SET NAME: Cole Mini
Dragon, Misfortune's Keep
SET NUMBER: 70599,
70605
YEAR: 2016

Pirate head scarf
matches Sqiffy's,
but worn at a
different angle.

Makeshift eye
patch covers
Bucko's left eye.

DID YOU KNOW?
Bucko's real name is
Landon. But like Colin,
Nadakhan didn't think it
was a good pirate
name, so he
changed it.

Orange is
Bucko's
favorite
color!

BLADE BATTLES
Bucko is a skilled swordsman,
but he's happy to use any weapon
to hand in a battle. Here he has a
strong hold on a Djinn Blade, so the
ninja will have to fight hard to take
it from him.

Djinn Blade
with white
and blue
attachments

THE FIERY, RED-BEARDED BUCKO is
another new recruit to Nadakhan's pirate
crew. He is a strong and a fearless fighter
and follows orders without question—just
the kind of shipmate that Nadakhan likes.
Bucko is more than eager to do the
manipulative Djinn's dirty work.

ON TIGER WIDOW ISLAND:

FIGHT OFF ATTACKING SKY PIRATES

BEWARE: POISONOUS SPIDERS!

FIND A SAFE CAVE TO HIDE IN

WATCH OUT FOR FALLING COCONUTS

BEHIND THE BRICKS

DK SPOKE TO THE LEGO® NINJAGO™ team to find out the secrets behind making the enduringly popular LEGO sets, minifigures, and TV show, and to discover what's coming up next for everybody's favourite ninja! Design Director Simon Lucas heads the team, Nicolaas Johan Bernardo Vás is a LEGO NINJAGO model designer, and Daniel McKenna is a graphic designer, specializing in minifigures—including the exclusive that comes with the trade edition of this book.

LEGO® INTERVIEW: SIMON LUCAS

Can you tell us about your role within the LEGO® NINJAGO™ team?

As Design Director, I am responsible for the LEGO® NINJAGO™ products and get to lead a team of talented LEGO designers. The design team and I work on all the concepts for the LEGO sets, minifigure characters and also the TV series—NINJAGO™: Masters of Spinjitzu. My role definitely goes "beyond the brick", as I am heavily involved in the story and production of the TV series. I joined The LEGO Group in 2011 as a Senior Designer and the first sets I worked on were LEGO® Hero Factory buildable action figures. I later became the creative lead for LEGO® Castle. In 2012, I became creative lead for LEGO NINJAGO and now as Design Director, I oversee all aspects of NINJAGO.

Simon Lucas is Design Director of the LEGO NINJAGO team. DK last interviewed him for DK's LEGO NINJAGO *Visual Dictionary*.

Have you always been a LEGO fan?

I was definitely a "LEGO Kid"! The biggest memory for me is of LEGO Pirates sets in the late 1980's and also the LEGO space sets. I also remember buying LEGO® Technic sets, which taught me a lot about engineering and how mechanisms work.

How did you go about planning the most recent season of LEGO NINJAGO?

For NINJAGO bad guys, we always want to create cool characters with a twist. For 2016, we started with something as iconic and classic as pirates and then gave it a NINJAGO fantasy twist by taking the pirates to the skies to create NINJAGO Sky Pirates. We really wanted to design a really diverse crew of crooks and scoundrels for the Sky Pirates, where the characters have lots of depth and backstory.

Do you have any favorite models or sets? If so, why?

In my last interview for DK, I said that the Destiny's Bounty (set 9446) was one of my favourite sets. But one of our newer sets The Temple of Airjitzu (set 70751) is my current favourite. It's a beautiful building that is classic NINJAGO. It is the biggest LEGO NINJAGO set we have ever done and has great features, like a working shadow puppet theatre.
Another recent favorite of mine is Attack of the Morro Dragon (set 70736). It's a new style of dragon for NINJAGO, where we have given it a scary ghost look and feel.

Are there any new or exclusive parts or pieces that you had to design? For example, the Ghost Ninja's translucent legs and tails?

It sounds easy but it was actually quite difficult to make transparent legs on the minifigures. Our production machines use lasers to recognise the minifigure torsos and legs and to begin with, it was difficult for the lasers to see the minifigure legs as the laser would just go straight through them. It was important for us to find a solution though because when we tested the ghost concept with kids they told us that ghosts are definitely see-through so therefore couldn't have solid legs. We eventually found a solution and these are the first LEGO minifigures to have two transparent legs! (One transparent leg more than previous LEGO® Legends of CHIMA™ characters.)

Also new for the ghost season were the ghost ninja hoods, featuring green ghostly energy coming out of the back. To create these new elements, they were molded using two colours in a very technical process at the LEGO Group known as 2K— meaning 2 component. The "K"' is because "component" in Danish is "komponent."

How do you plan what's next for LEGO NINJAGO? Is there anything coming up that you're excited about and can tell us about?

The LEGO NINJAGO design team works 18 months ahead. For us, the bad guy minifigures are always a good starting point. The ninja are well-established, so we first try to design cool, new bad guys. We show the designs to kids to see who is the coolest in their eyes.

After the ghost series, we thought about continuing with more ghosts, but pirates in the sky seemed newer, cooler, and allowed us to tell even more stories. There's a lot to be excited about in NINJAGO's future—like new bad guys and new stories—but for now, it's all top-secret!

Is there any element or character not yet in LEGO form that you would love to design?

We would love to be able to make more fan-favorites from the TV series into LEGO sets. For example, I would really like to be able to make all versions of the ninja that have only ever been in the TV series—such as when the ninja had to wear Master Wu's Tea shop outfits. It would be really cool to be able to collect them all.

There are also lots of funny background characters that have been developed for the TV series and never made into a real minifigure. For example, the tea-shop owner Mystake and Jay's mum and dad.

LEGO® INTERVIEW: NICOLAAS VAS AND DANIEL MCKENNA

Can you tell us about your roles within the LEGO® NINJAGO™ team?

Nicolaas: I help come up with ideas for creatures, buildings, vehicles, dragons, and the bad guys—and then bring it all to life with bricks.

Daniel: As graphic design lead I work with the creative leads and the designers to come up with characters and explore the concepts that we're creating. If we have a new concept—for example ninja fighting against ghosts—then I help to come up with new outfits for the ninja and then help to incorporate this into the bigger story.

How did you come to work at the LEGO Group?

N: I came to the LEGO Group in 2014. I definitely had a background as a LEGO fan—I built a lot of LEGO sets as a kid, in particular from the LEGO® Bionicle range, and didn't really stop.

D: I started working in Billund as a graphic designer four years ago. I used to work at LEGOLAND® California, where I built, amongst other things, large buildings and cars in the area called Miniland. I've pretty much been building with LEGO bricks my entire life. My favorites were the 1989 LEGO® Space Police and the sub-theme M-tron.

Nicolaas Vás is a LEGO NINJAGO Model Designer.

How do you come to plan upcoming LEGO sets and minifigures? For the LEGO NINJAGO range, the storyline plays such a huge part—how do you keep everything exciting and fresh?

N: We start by thinking about the bad guys—how do we make a bigger enemy for the ninja to face, for example, with more imposing elements.

D: One of the hardest parts is finding novelty while making sure that the ninja still look like the ninja that the kids know and love. We try to incorporate new elements—for example, the Anacondrai wear basic armour, but with leather and woven elements, and the Skybound outfits we designed to be a bit more steampunk, but also pilot style.

Did you design any brand-new elements for the Sky Pirates theme?

N: This year we featured balloon elements in a LEGO NINJAGO set for the first time. This element was already existing but quite new generally and it was fun to take aviation parts but mix them up with traditional pirate parts— such as the anchors and the helm wheel piece. We took and reinvented a lot of traditional nautical elements.

D: We always try to reuse elements and come up with something new. This year we have our first LEGO NINJAGO "bigfig" in Dogshank, which is really exciting. We also have a new sword hilt element for the pirate minifigures, which has a combined stud and click function. The pirate swords also have a skull attached to make them seem "piratey," while the ninja have new two-color helmets and shoulder armor. The single pauldron design makes fighting easier but still manages to hold two katanas, mounted on one side. This new look is, we think, more swashbuckling!

Do you have a favorite LEGO NINJAGO set or minifigure?

Nicolaas: My favorite model is the Temple of Airjitzu (set 70751). Adrian on our team did a fantastic job with all of the architectural details and it was great to be able to contribute in a small way to such a big set. All six of the ninja are included in this set, together for the first time ever, and in a more peaceful environment for a change. This set is all about them having fun and experiencing day-to-day life. Also for the Sky Pirates sets, it's been really cool to be able to bring back a LEGO monkey and make it robotic.

Daniel: I was most excited to work on Skylor's minifigure. This was the first female ninja that we designed. We all tried to figure out what she would look like as we weren't sure if she would be a bad guy. I like that we now have a yellow-orange colored ninja as it really completes the rainbow range of ninja.

What's next for LEGO NINJAGO? What would you personally really love to design?

N: There are a lot of really cool locations from the TV series that it would be good to revisit in physical LEGO form. There are a lot of cool ninja bases that have been seen in the show. We love making new locations but it would also be great to revisit old ones.

D: Two characters that I'd love to make (although we'd have to find the right way to fit them into the story) are Nya in her civilian teacher's outfit from the "Rebooted" series and Zane in his pink outfit after Lloyd pulls a prank on him with his laundry and dyes it all pink.

There are also lots of fan-favourite Elemental Tournament Masters from all over Ninjago Island that we'd love to see back—for example, Ash and Bolobo.

Daniel McKenna is a graphic designer on the LEGO® NINJAGO™ team. Here he holds the exclusive Jay minifigure that he helped to design for the trade edition of this book.

How did you come to choose the exclusive minifigure for this book?

D: We approach exclusive minifigures differently to those in the playtheme, which matches up to the TV series. After the "Rebooted" season in 2014 we saw the perfect opportunity to launch this armored version of Jay. We were matching the style of armor as worn on the Stone Warrior armor minifigure variants of Lloyd, Kai, and Zane, but we got to design extra leg print, which is not seen on the TV show. Each ninja has a variant of the armor look to make them more individual.

This is the first appearance of a new double-sided head design for Jay: confident expression on one side, with the worried expression often seen on the TV series on the other. And adding the comic book element was Nicolaas's idea!

Design Director Simon Lucas adds: Jay is going to be the lead character in the Sky Pirates series—this is his moment in the sun and (spoilers!) he will ultimately save the day. This Jay minifigure is wearing his silver Stone Warrior armor – all of the ninja have been seen wearing this special armor in Episode 34—"The Titanium Ninja"—in the TV show, but only Lloyd, Kai and Zane have worn it in physical minifigure form in LEGO sets. We know that kids love to collect all the special armor variants so we saw this as the perfect opportunity.

The tile accompanying Jay reads "Starfarer", which is Jay's favourite comic, featuring his hero Fritz Donnegen—a fictional action hero. This comic has also appeared in the TV show—in the comic-book store—and Lloyd is also a fan.

SET GALLERY

HERE ARE ALL THE LEGO®
NINJAGO™ sets produced so far in
each series. How many sets have you
collected? Which is your favorite?

2505
Garmadon's Dark Fortress

2506
Skull Truck

2507
Fire Temple

2508
Blacksmith Shop

2254
Mountain Shrine

2258
Ninja Ambush

2509
Earth Dragon Defense

2516
Ninja Training Outpost

2260
Ice Dragon Attack

2259
Skull Motorbike

2518
Nuckal's ATV

2519
Skeleton Bowling

2263
Turbo Shredder

2504
Spinjitzu Dojo

2520
Ninjago Battle Arena

2521
Lightning Dragon Battle

TV PILOT : NINJA VS. SKELETONS

9440
Venomari Shrine

9441
Kai's Blade Cycle

9450
Epic Dragon Battle

9455
Fangpyre Mech

9442
Jay's Storm Fighter

9443
Rattlecopter

9456
Spinner Battle

9457
Fangpyre Wrecking Ball

9444
Cole's Tread Assault

9445
Fangpyre Truck Ambush

9446
Destiny's Bounty

9447
Lasha's Bite Cycle

9448
Samurai Mech

9449
Ultra Sonic Raider

IT'S BITE VS. MIGHT!

Help the ninja to take the Fangpyre Fang Blade back from Pythor in Ultra Sonic Raider (set 9949).

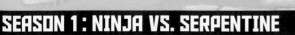

SEASON 1: NINJA VS. SERPENTINE

70500
Kai's Fire Mech

70501
Warrior Bike

70720
Hover Hunter

70721
Kai Fighter

70502
Cole's Earth Driller

70503
The Golden Dragon

70722
OverBorg Attack

70723
Thunder Raider

70504
Garmatron

70505
Temple of Light

70724
NinjaCopter

70725
Nindroid MechDragon

70726
Destructoid

70727
Ninja Charger

70728
Battle for Ninjago City

5002144
Dareth vs. Nindroid

850632
Samurai Accessory Set

70745
Anacondrai Crusher

70746
Condrai Copter Attack

70756
Dojo Showdown

30291
Anacondrai
Battle Mech

70747
Boulder Blaster

70748
Titanium Dragon

30292
Jay Nano Mech

30293
Kai Drifter

70749
Enter the Serpent

70750
Ninja DB X

LET'S
SHOOT SOME
SNAKES!

70752
Jungle Trap

70753
Lava Falls

70754
ElectroMech

70755
Jungle Raider

Join the fight with Nya's detachable flyer featuring
stud-shooters in NINJA DBX (set 70750).

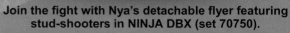

SEASON 4 : NINJA VS. MASTER CHEN AND HIS ANACONDRAI ARMY

70730
Chain Cycle Ambush

70731
Jay Walker One

70739
Airjitzu Kai Flyer

70740
Airjitzu Jay Flyer

70732
City of Stiix

70733
Blaster Bike

70741
Airjitzu Cole Flyer

70742
Airjitzu Zane Flyer

70734
Master Wu Dragon

70735
Ronin R.E.X

70743
Airjitzu Morro Flyer

70744
Airjitzu Wrayth Flyer

70736
Attack of the Morro Dragon

70737
Titan Mech Battle

30294
The Cowler Dragon

851342
Battle Pack

70738
Final Flight of Destiny's Bounty

70751
Temple of Airjitzu

SEASON 5 : NINJA VS. GHOST ARMY

70599
Cole's Dragon

70600
Ninja Bike Chase

70601
Sky Pirate Jet

70602
Jay's Elemental Dragon

70603
Raid Zeppelin

70604
Tiger Widow Island

70605
Misfortune's Keep

Soar above Ninjago Island with Master Wu
in his hot-air balloon in Raid Zeppelin
(set 70603).

SEASON 6 : NINJA VS. SKY PIRATES

Project Editor Emma Grange
Senior Designer Jo Connor
Editor Arushi Vats
Designers Radhika Banerjee, Dimple Vohra
Editorial Assistants Beth Davies, Rosie Peet
Pre-Production Producer Marc Staples
Senior Producer Lloyd Robertson
Editorial Managers Paula Regan, Simon Hugo,
Chitra Subramanyam
Design Managers Guy Harvey, Neha Ahuja
Art Director Lisa Lanzarini
Publisher Julie Ferris
Publishing Director Simon Beecroft

First American Edition, 2016
Published in the United States by DK Publishing
345 Hudson Street, New York, NY 10014

Page design Copyright © 2016 Dorling Kindersley Limited
DK, a Division of Penguin Random House LLC

16 17 18 19 20 10 9 8 7 6 5 4 3 2 1
001-280773-Jun/16

DK books are available at special discounts when purchased in bulk for sales
promotions, premiums, fund-raising, or educational use. For details, contact: DK
Publishing Special Markets, 345 Hudson Street, New York, New York 10014
SpecialSales@dk.com

Printed and bound in China

ACKNOWLEDGMENTS
DK would like to thank Randi Sørensen, Martin Leighton Lindhart, Paul Hansford,
Madeline Boushie, Simon Lucas, Nicolaas Johan Bernardo Vás, and Daniel
McKenna at the LEGO Group, Gary Ombler for extra photography, Andy Jones
for extra editorial help, Sam Bartlett for design assistance, and Claire Sipi for
her writing. For the original edition of this book, DK would like to thank
Shari Last, Julia March, Ruth Amos, Lauren Rosier, Mark Richards, Jon Hall,
Clive Savage, Ron Stobbart, and Catherine Saunders.

A WORLD OF IDEAS:
SEE ALL THERE IS TO KNOW

www.dk.com
www.LEGO.com